BHAVARTHA RATNAKARA

Bhavartha Ratnakara

BANGALORE VENKATA RAMAN

GAYATRI DEVI VASUDEV

MOTILAL BANARSIDASS INTERNATIONAL
DELHI

Reprint Edition : Delhi, 2025
Twelfth Edition : 1995

© MOTILAL BANARSIDASS INTERNATIONAL
All Rights Reserved

ISBN : 978-81-19394-24-1 (PB)
ISBN : 978-81-19394-55-5 (HB)

Also available at
MOTILAL BANARSIDASS INTERNATIONAL
H.O. : 41 U.A. Bungalow Road, (Back Lane)Jawahar Nagar, Delhi - 110 007
4261 (basement) Lane #3,Ansari Road, Darya Ganj, New Delhi - 110 002
203 Royapettah High Road, Mylapore, Chennai - 600 004
12/1A, 2nd Floor, Bankim Chatterjee Street, Kolkata - 700 073
Stockist : Motilal Books, Ashok Rajpath, Near Kali Mandir, Patna - 800 004

No part of this book may be reproduced in any form or by any electronic
or mechanical means including information storage and retrieval systems
without permission in writing from the publishers, excepts by a reviewer
who may quote brief passages in a review.

Printed in India
MOTILAL BANARSIDASS INTERNATIONAL

Contents

Foreword .... (vii)
Preface to the Seventh Edition .... (ix)
Preface .... (xi)
Introduction .... (xiii)

1. Lagna or First House 1
   Mesha Lagna 1
   Vrishabha Lagna 12
   Mithuna Lagna 19
   Karkataka Lagna 22
   Simha Lagna 26
   Kanya Lagna 29
   Thula Lagna 32
   Vrischika Ascendant 39
   Dhanur Lagna 42
   Makara Lagna 44
   Kumbha Lagna 47
   Meena Lagna 50

2. **Dhana Yogas** 55
   Nirdhana Yogas 61
   Combinations for Poverty 61
   Education 65
   On Tastes or Flavours 74

3. Brothers 80

4. Conveyances and Fortune 84

5. Enemies and Diseases 93

6. Seventh House Indications 97
7. Health and Longevity 102
8. Fortunate Combinations 109
9. Raja Yogas 119
   Combinations for Dips in Sacred Waters 133
10. Combinations for Death 136
11. Results of Dasas 145
12. Ordinary Combinations 158
13. Graha Malika Yogas 166
14. Planetary Rulerships, etc. 179
Index of Technical Terms 187

Foreword

Interest in astrology is growing in leaps and bounds all over the world as both individuals and countries realize its importance in handling difficult situations that defy all efforts and common sense. Astrology can provide very good insights that can help both nations and individuals deal with such situations but this subject has never been properly presented. The present work by my revered father and the doyen of astrology Dr. B.V. Raman, though written in the 1930's, is still very relevant to the present times and covers the ancient yet modern science of Jyotisha in a concise and comprehensive manner introducing the astrology-enthusiast to the wide range of topics that comprise Jyotisha.

Useful information and planetary details in interpreting a horoscope, whether of an individual or of a nation, have been included in these pages. Both the beginner as well as the advanced student of science will find all the details needed for methodically deciphering the future given in this title.

I thank Mr. J.P. Jain and Mr. Abhishek Jain of M/s. Motilal Banarsidass International for bringing out this edition after a hiatus of many years.

Bangalore **Gayatri Devi Vasudev**
December 7, 2023

Preface to the Seventh Edition

Though the sixth edition went out of print a year ago, the seventh edition could not be published earlier due to my other heavy lecture and research preoccupations.

The seventh edition, now presented before the educated public is free from some typographical errors found in the previous editions.

It is hoped that *Bhavartha Ratnakara* will be great use to all lovers of astrology, amateurs and professionals, and that it will be received with enthusiasm by my esteemed readers.

Bangalore   **B. V. RAMAN**
16-12-1977

Preface

Shine inward, and the mind through all her powers
Irradiate there plant eyes, all mist from thence
Purge and disperse that I may see and tell of things
invisible to mortal sight.

MILTON

Astrology holds a prominent place in the life of every Indian. No important work is done or activity undertaken without first consulting the horoscope. When such is the case it behaves on every thinking individual to maintain the dignity and purity of the science by insisting on the necessity of a systematic study of the subject on rational and *approved lines. Such a study is possible only when standard* books are published. In the present day, the subject is so mishandled and misused by ignorant and ill informed astrologers that *each* Tom, Dick and Harry call himself an astrologer and some of the credulous public fall an easy prey to the snares set up by such quacks. The educated public will do well to study the general principles of the science so that if at all they wish to consult an astrologer, such knowledge might guide them to select the right sort of person. It is with a view to enabling the educated public to have an insight into the general principles astrology that this translation is presented *Bhavartha of Ratnakara* is a short treatise on astrology, composed by the great Ramanuja and the way the different principles are presented by the author will not fail to make a powerful impression on the minds of the readers.

I have not simply given the translation leaving the readers to seek their own explanations of difficult principles and combinations. I have tried to explain the difficulties as best as I could by way of notes in appropriate places and by way of examples where such examples are needed. I am sure this work will be liked by my readers just as all my other books have been liked and appreciated by them.

I must express my obligations to the great Sanskrit scholar of the old orthodox type (for whose knowledge I have great regard) who helped me to decipher some of the difficult stanzas but who has preferred to remain anonymous.

Bangalore   **B. V. RAMAN,** M.R.A.S.,
4-3-1944   *Editor The Astrological Magazine*

Introduction

BHAVARTHA RATNAKARA is a treatise on astrology said to have been written by Sri Ramanujacharya and it deals with subject in a masterly way. The translation notes and examples I have given in these pages will speak for themselves. Several books have been written by me on astrology — some of them compilations and some of them products of my researches in the field of practical astrology. I have always felt that the real astrological truths lay hidden in the Sanskrit language and the only way to bring them to the notice of the general public is to render them into English and explain the principles to the best of my humble ability and experience. My grand father late Prof. B Suryanarain Rao has done into English some of the most important work such as *Brihat Jathaha, Sarwatha Chintamani Jamini Sutras* etc., and his translations have been immensely liked by the educated public not only for the clarity with which difficult Sanskrit terms have been put into plain English but also for the vast practical experience he has brought to bear upon the inimitable notes he has given. There are a number of books extant in Sanskrit on astrology and I pitched my attention on this particular book because I found that the several combinations mentioned in it are not only useful and workable in actual practice but the entire subject of astrology has been dealt with systematically and yet concisely. I had decided to bring out a translation of this book three years ago but had to put off the decision as I wanted to test the various principles rather exhaustively by applying them to practical horoscopes before I could bring them to the notice of the public.

The difficulties of a translator are indeed many. Prof. Rao's introduction to *Sarwatha Chinthamani* will make clear the pitfalls in the way of a translator. Firstly he should be well versed in the subject he wishes to interpret. Secondly he should possess a good knowledge of the language into which he intends the translation to be made. Thirdly in subject like astrology, mere scholarship and linguistic ability alone are not sufficient to make one a successful translator. He should possess vast practical experience which would enable him to appreciate how far a given combination can be made use of to suit different nativities. Fourthly the flexibility of the *Sanskrit* language has been a great stumbling block in the way of rightly understanding the technical terms. Take the following verse and see whether the head or the tail of it can be made even by an expert in Sanskrit language unless he knows the key.

मा मा सौ मारि रम्भ
(MA MA SAW MARI RAMBHA)

The principles of astrology are couched in symbolic language and one not familiar with these technicalities would only get confounded. The above line gives the friendships, enmities, etc, for the Sun while a literal rendering would give a hotch potch meaning.

Astrology is purely a technical subject and no amount of mere scholarship in English or in Sanskrit would be any use unless one is thoroughly familiar with important principles of the science. The translator's responsibility rests more upon conveying the spirit of the original writer than upon simply interpreting the stanzas word by word. In other words the translation must be liberal rather than literal.

Moreover, a translation devoid of suitable explanations, examples and notes will not serve the purpose for which it is intended. Translation means the interpretation put upon the author by the translator and not the original forcible expression of the author. Therefore the difficulties of a translator are real and not imaginary.

In my translation of this work, I have endevoured to be as faithful to the original as possible not losing sight of the fact that the spirit of the author should be conveyed to the readers rather than a verbatim rendering or word to word translation. Some scholars seem to believe that they will have rendered a great service to astrology if they publish literal translations of the original Sanskrit works. They would even translate the name of the author such as for instance Kesava Daivagna as Kesava the astrologer, ignoring the fact that the words Daivagna, Sastri, etc, are used as suffixes after the name.

I Shall now say something about the work under consideration and its author. The book is divided into 14 *Tarangas* or Chapters. The total number of stanzas is 384, the first chapter being the largest containing 130 stanzas and the 5th Chapter being the smallest containing only 8 stanzas. Almost all Sanskrit books deal with the essentials of astrology in the first chapter while this author has consigned the elementary principles to the last one. The First

Chapter begins with a delineation of favorable and unfavorable dispositions of planets for persons born in different Ascendants. The author has made some departures at certain places from the cannons of Parasari – meaning the principles of astrology as current now. For instance while dealing with Vrishaba Ascendant he says that Saturn is not a Yogakaraka for Taurus in spite of the fact that he owns the 9th and 10th houses. I have tried to explain such departures in the notes to the appropriate stanzas. The Second Chapter deals with *Dhana Yogas* (combinations for wealth), *Nirdhana Yogas* (combinations for poverty), *Vidya* (education) and *Bhukthi* (tastes) contains 33 stanzas Chapter Three deals with brothers, (*Bhrathru*) in the course of 10 stanzas while the Fourth Chapter gives a fairly exhaustive treatment of *Vahana bhagya Yoga* (combinations for possessing conveyances and general fortune). Incidentally two stanzas dispose off the fifth house. The sixth house com- prehending enemies and diseases (*Satruroga*) is discussed in the Fifth Chapter in the course of 8 stanzas while the 7th house forms the subject matter of the 13 stanzas composing the Sixth Chapter. Health and longevity (*Ayurarogya*) is disposed off in the couse of 13 stanzas in the Seventh Chapter while the ninth house indications going under the general term of Fortunate Combinatins (*BhagyaYoga*) are dealt with in the Eighth Chapter. The Ninth Chapter contains 29 stanzas and deals with *Raja Yoga* and *PunyaYoga*. The Tenth Chapter, devoted to *Maraka* or death, gives a numer of important combinations which enable one to predict the periods and sub periods under which one's death is likely to happen. The Eleventh Chapter gives information about the results of Dasa (*Mahadasaphala*). The principles adumbrated here are no doubt consistent with the general cannons of Parasari system, but certain combinations appear to be apparently contradictory and not explainable according to the general rules of Dasa interpretation. I have found such combinations workable in the majority of cases in actual practice. To give an illustration, Stanza 26 of the Eleventh Chapter suggests that one becomes timid in the course of Rahu Dasa if Mercury is in the 3rd house. What Rahu has to do with Mercury in such a combination I cannot say. The third is the house of courage and Mercury being an important planet, his situation in the third indicates want of courage. But why during the Dasa of Rahu, the subject should lose courage when Mercury is in the third is not understandable. You will however find that even the most courageous person becomes somewhat timid in the bhukthi of Mercury during Rahu Dasa. This, of course is my own observation. The Twelfth Chapter deals with "Ordinary Combinations" (*Grahasamanya Yoga*) and gives combinations which would add vitality to the various bhavas and which would render the bhavas week. The Thirteenth Chapter deals of *Malika Yoga* or combinations which would be formed by the disposition of planets in the fashion of a garland or wreath commencing from the Ascendant and different houses. The last or Fourteenth Chapter gives the elements of astrology such as planetary ownerships, exaltations, friendships, enmities etc., Thus it will be seen that the author has surveyed the entire field of *phalabhaga* or predictive astrology in a comprehensive and yet concise manner, his treatment of certain bhavas such as the fifth house being rather meagre.

As regards the author, his parentage and his place, the only evidence available are the two stanzas following the invocation at the beginning of the book and the concluding part of each chapter from which we gather the information that he is the son of Sree Bhasyam Jagannatharya (who is highly learned in astrology, a gem among scholars and well versed in Agamas) residing in the Mahakshetra of Mangaladri and belonging to the Bharadvaja gotra. The name of the author is given at the end of each chapter as Sree Ramanujacharya, who I am inclined to think is none other than the great Visishttadwarta philosopher. It is a fashion with many of the oriental scholars – both Indian and European – to laugh at the suggestion that astrological works were also composed by poets like Kalidasa and Acharyas like Sankara and Ramanuja Kalidasa the great poet and dramatist has written the famous *Jyotirvidabharana* and *Uttarakalamrita*, masterpieces on the astrological science, in addition to the achievements in the field of drama. In *Jyotirvidabharana* he has given a description of the fleet of Vikramaditya the Great whose contemporary he was and which fact has been made clear by the following stanza (*Vide* Jyotirvidabharana).

"DHANUANTHARIH KSHAPANAKOMARASIMHA SANKU BHOTHALABHATTA GHATAKARPARA KALIDASAH"

"KHYATHO VARAHANIHIRO NRIPATHADSSADHAYAM VAIVARARUCHIRNAVA VIKRAMASYA"

Yet Dr Keru, the editor 'Bibliothica Indica Series in the introduction he has given to Varahamihira's *Brihat Samhita*, denies the fact of Kalidasa and Vikramaditya having been contemporaries and interlaces a pseudo Kalidasa whenever facts do not fit into his pet

Introduction   xix

theories and prejudices. Of course for him the usual authorities are Wilson, Weber & Co. and not the great Indian scholars of the orthodox type who alone are competent to speak on such subjects bearing on Indian History, Philosophy and Sciences. The great Advaita philosopher Sankaracharya has no doubt produced the most valuable treatises by way of commentaries on Vedas and Upanishads, but he has also written books on astrology and astronomy. For instance the famous astronomical work "Kacharadarpana" is said to have been written by the great Sankaracharya. When we have in our own times people who can claim proficiency in more than one, subject it is no wonder that master minds like Kalidasa, Sankara, Ramanuja and Varahamihira who were versatile geniuses could write with authority on more than one subject. Thus it will be seen that when the authorship of "Bhavartha Rathnakara" is attributed to Sree Ramanujacharya, as is evident from the closing part of each chapter, it is no wonder that the said Ramanujacharya could be none other than the great Visishtadwaita philosopher. Prejudices play a great part in suppressing truth and especially, when one has to deal with a subject like astrology, one's prejudices (unless one is really broadminded and cares for nothing but truth) will have free vent.

Until the contrary is proved there is no harm in accepting the fact brought out in each chapter that "Bhavartha Ratnakara is written by the great Ramanujacharya.

I have tried to be as simple and clear as possible both in my translation, and explanation and I am sure readers will like the translation, especially because I have tried to incorporate into the notes the experience, humble as it may be I have gathered both in my study and practice during the last sixteen years of my labours in this field.

I have only one request to make before my readers and that is if you find any mistakes or omissions in my translation and notes and if you have any reasonable and constructive criticism to offer bring them to my notice and I shall rectify them in the next edition.

I shall feel myself rewarded if readers find the book interesting and instructive.

Bangalore   **B. V. RAMAN**
04-03-1944   M.R.A.S.

। श्रीरस्तु ॥
॥ श्री मद्रामानुजाय नमः ॥
ज्योतिःशास्त्र भावार्थरत्नाकरः ।

अध लग्नतरंगः ।

Chapter 1

Lagna or First House

मेषलग्न विचारः
MESHA LAGNA

मेषलग्ने तु जातस्य राजयोगीऽपि लभ्यते ।
चतुर्थप चमाधीश संबन्धेन न संशयः ॥ १ ॥

Stanza 1. For a person born in Mesha Ascendant, Raja Yoga will undoubtedly result by the combination of the lords of 4th and 5th houses.

मेषलग्ने तु जातस्य धनसप्तमनायकः ।
शुक्रः करोति निधनमिति ज्योतिषकाविदुः ॥ २ ॥

Stanza 2. Astrologers opine that for a person born in Mesha Ascendant. Venus lord of the 2nd and 7th will become a Maraka.

मेषलग्ने तु जातस्य भाग्यान्त्यस्थान नायकः ।
देवेन्द्रपूज्यो राज्यस्थ सभवेन्मारक स्मृतः॥ ३ ॥

Stanza 3. For a Mesha Ascendant person, Jupiter, lord of the 9th and 12th, becomes a Maraka if he occupies the 10th house.

मेषलग्ने तु जातस्य राजयोगो न लभ्यते ।
भाग्यराज्येश संबधमात्रेणहि न संशयः ॥ ४ ॥

Stanza 4. For a person born in Mesha Ascendant the merc combination of the lords of the 9th and 10th viz., Jupiter and Saturn does not result in Raja Yoga: This is certain.

NOTES

The author's treatment of the subject is quite comprehensive, interesting and unique. The first four stranzas make clear the following points in respect of persons born in Mesha Ascendant.

1. Raja Yoga is caused by the mere combination of the lords of the 4th and 5th, viz., the Moon and the Sun.

The nature of the Raja Yoga, the extent of its influence and other similar details are not elaborated by the author so that much skill and experience are necessary on the part of the reader who wishes to apply the principles to actual horoscopes.

2. Venus lord of the 2nd and 7th becomes a Maraka.

Parasara says that because Venus happens to be lord of the 2nd and 7th he cannot himself become capable of inflicting death but can become a Maraka only when he is in conjunction with other Marakas such as Mercury and Saturn as Keraleeya also gives expression to Parasara's view when it observes thus *Shukrassakshannahanthasy adithikeralamruaya* meaning that Sukra by himself cannot become a Maraka. In my humble experience I have been able to come across a number of cases in which persons born into Mesh Ascendant have died in the course of Sukra Dasa.

Lagna or First House

3. Jupiter, lord of the 9th and 12th can become a Maraka if he occupies the 10th house.

It is not clear as to why the author inclines to the view that Jupiter can become a Maraka only when he is in the 10th house. Probably the author feels that because Jupiter becomes neecha (debilitated) in the 10th from Mesha he loses all benefic influences. Parasara on the other hand says that the Sun and Jupiter are benefics for Mesha Ascendant Keraleeya says that Mercury and Saturn become Marakas for Mesha Ascendant. It will be seen that an examination of a number of horoscopes reveals that Mercury is the determinant of death as he is lord of the 3rd and 6th.

Chart No. 1—*Born on 5-3-1898 at about 9 a.m., L.M.T. Lat. 13° N., Long. 77° 35' E.*

	Lagna					Sun	Jupiter Venus
Merc. Sun Venus	RASI		Kethu Moon	Merc. Rahu	NAVAMSA		Lagna
Mars Rahu				Saturn			Mars Kethu
	Saturn		Jupit.		Moon		

Balance of Saturn's Dasa at birth: years 2-3-19

In Chart No 1 death occurred in the 20th year of the native, in the major period of Mercury Mercury's power to kill has been fortified by his conjunction with Venus.

4. The mere combination of Jupiter and Saturn lords of 9th and 10th does not result in Raja Yoga.

This view is also supported by the great Parasara when he says that good will not be produced when Jupiter and Saturn are in conjunction.

न शुभम् योगमात्रेण प्रवदेत् शनिजीवयो: ।

For Mesha Ascendant though Saturn is lord of the 10th he stands blemished because he is also the 11th lord. The evil is strong enough to vitiate Jupiter the 9th lord when be happens to be associated with 11th Lord. Hence the association of Saturn with Jupiter will not confer any Yoga.

Chart No. 2—*Born on 13-10-1860 at about 7 p.m., L.M.T. Lat. 13° N., Long. 77° 35' E.*

	Lagna			Rahu	Jupit.	Mars Moon
		RASI		Merc.	NAVAMSA	
Mars			Jupit. Saturn			Venus Saturn
		Merc.	Venus Sun Moon		Lagna	Kethu Sun

Balance of Saturn's Dasa at birth: years 6-1-28

In Chart No. 2 the native lost his appointment in Guru Dasa Saturn bhukti though both are placed in the 5th house aspected by exalted Mars. However in Mercury's sub period, the position was regained while death also took place at the end of Mercury.

मेषलग्ने तु जातस्य स्फोट शस्त्रव्रणादिनम् ।
भयमस्ति च जगु: प्रायशो गणिकोत्तमा: ॥ ५॥

Lagna or First House

Stanza 5. A person born when Mesha is rising will have fear from small pox, weapons and wounds. So say the learned (in astrology).

षष्ठभाष्टमनाथेन युतो भूमिसुतो यदि ।
तद्दशान्तर्दशाकाले निधनम् मूर्ध्नि कृन्तनम्ः ॥ ६ ॥

Stanza 6. If Mars is in conjunction with 6th and 8th lords, death, occurs in the course of his Dasa and Bhukthi by diseases pertaining to the head.

मेषे जातस्य धनपो व्ययस्थोऽपि कविश्शुभः ।
इतरक्षे तु जातस्य व्ययस्थ धनपोऽशुभः ॥ ७ ॥

Stanza 7. For one born in Mesha, if the lord of the 2nd is in the 12th, he becomes good. For those born in other Ascendants the 2nd lord does not become good if he is placed in the 12th.

मेषे जातस्य भौमस्तु शुक्रेण सहितो यदि ।
योगदो भविता भूयो मारकोऽपि भवेदसौ ॥ ८ ॥

Stanza 8. For .one born in Mesha Ascendant Mars no doubt becomes a Maraka if he is in conjunction with Venus, but still he will be capable of causing Yoga also.

मेषे जातस्य भौमस्तु गुरूशुक्रसमन्वितः ।
द्वितीये यदि विद्येत योगदो भवति ध्रुवम् ॥ ९ ॥

Stanza 9. For a person born in Mesha langna Mars will certainly become a Yoga Karaka (conferer of fame) if he occupies the 2nd house with Jupiter and Venus.

मेषे जातस्य भौमस्तु गुरूशुक्रसमन्वितः ।
तृतीयस्थो यदि भवेन्नैव योगप्रदो भवेत् ॥ १० ॥

Stanza 10. For one born in Mesha Ascendant, Mars does not produce any Yoga if he occupies the 3rd house with Jupiter and Venus.

मेषे जातस्य भौमस्तु गुरूणा च समन्वितः ।
चतुर्थस्थो यदि भवेद्योगदो भवति ध्रुवम् ॥ ११ ॥

Stanza 11. Mars will surely become a Yogakaraka for one who take his birth in Mesha Ascendant, if he is in the 4th house combined with Jupiter.

मेषे जातस्य हि कुजः पचमस्थो भवेद्यदि ।
कुजदाये च संप्राप्ते योगदश्च भवेध्रुवम् ॥ १२ ॥

Stanza 12. For a person born in Mesha Ascendant, Mars in the 5th house surely causes Yoga in the course of his own dasa.

NOTES

In the above 8 slokas the author explains the various combinations which render Mars the lord Ascendant (*a*) capable of inflicting death and (*b*) capable of conferring Yoga or fame. Summarising the above we find that:

1. Death occurs in the Dasa of Mars by diseases pertaining to the head if Mars is associated with 6th and 8th lords

It is not clear as to what the author means when he refers to Mars being in association with 8th lord "SHASHTA-BHASHTAMANATHENA YUTHO BHUMI SUTHO YADI" Mars is himself the 8th lord for Mesha Ascendant. Consequently the 6th stanza should be taken to mean that when Mars conjoins the 6th lord, death will be caused in his Dasa. This combination is perfectly understandable because,

Lagna or First House

Mars though Lagnadhipathi can become a Maraka when he is in conjunction with the 6th lord (Mercury) who is also the lord of the 3rd.

2. Stanza 8 says that Mars becomes a Maraka, if he is in conjunction with Venus. But this does not prevent Mars from conferring Yoga also Chart No. 2 given above reveals that Mercury did not only give rise to good results during his bhukti, but inflicted death also. Similarly, as Lagnadhipathi, Mars can confer beneficial results while as lord of the 8th in conjunction with lord of the 7th he can cause death also. The way the various principles are enumerated clearly reveals the author's profound knowledge of the various technicalities of the astrological science.

3. Stanza 9 says that Mars can become Yogakaraka if he is in the 2nd with Jupiter and Venus, while the 10th stanza says that the above Yoga gets cancelled if the combination occurs in the 3rd house. Venus is lord of the 2nd while Jupiter is lord of the $9^{th,}$ Mars is lord of Ascendant. This combination of the lords of Ascendant, 2nd and 9th is certainly indicative of immense wealth and therefore Mars becomes a Yogakaraka. When this combination occurs in the 3rd house the potency is lost. It is also found from experience that during the Dasas of Mars, Jupiter and Venus, one suffers considerably from debts, enemies, litigation, loss of honour, misunderstandings, mental worry and diseases.

4. When Mars is in the 4th (Cancer) with Jupiter the former becomes quite capable of conferring Yoga. If in addition to Mars being in Cancer with Jupiter, the Moon is also there and if Mars is in the constellation of Alesha and Jupiter and the Moon are in Pushyami,

then the sub-period of the moon in Mars Dasa and *vice versa*, and the sub-period of the Moon in Jupiter Dasa and *vice versa* will confer Raja Yoga results. There will be access to wealth, lands houses, valuable acquaintances, realization of ambitions, honour from rulers, getting back the amounts lent, auspicious celebrations, access to power and similar favourable happenings. Between the Dasa of Moon and Mars, if the Moon is weak, *i.e.*, waning, then the above results will be conferred during Mars Dasa. If the Moon is more powerful, then the results will happen in Moon's Dasa. Between Moon and Jupiter, the latter would definitely be more favourable.

When Mars is in the 4th for a person born in Aries, the planet becomes debilitated. If Jupiter is in Cancer, where he will be exalted, the Neecha effect of Mars is cancelled with the result, Lagnadhipathi is subject to a distinct Neechabhanga Raja Yoga.

In all these case Mars seems to confer more of fame than of material possession or wealth. Humble as my experience has been, I have always found Mars making the native famous rather than rich.

5. According to Stanza 12 Mars confers fame in his Das if he is in the 5th.

The fifth is Leo or Simha — a friendly sign Lagnadhipathi in the 5th is always held to be good, though Parasara and Lomasa say that the native will not have much happiness from children and that the first child does not live "LAGNESA PANCHAMA MANEE SUTASOWKHYAMCHA MADHYAMAM PRADHAMAPATHYA NASASYAD KRODHI RAJAPRAVESAH".

Lagna or First House

Mars may become a Yogakaraka but may render the native unhappy in respect of children.

6. Stanza 7 reveals that only in regard to Mesha Ascendant lord of 2nd in the 12th is good. For other Ascendants such a disposition of the 2nd lord renders him evil.

This is an important principle worth noting and its rationale is perfectly understandable Lord of the 2nd from Mesha is Venus, when he is in the 12th or Pisces, he gets exalted and thereby the 2nd lord becomes strong.

मेषे जातस्य हि गुरूर्लाभस्थान स्थिवे भवेत् ।
गुरूर्द्दशायाम् संप्राप्ताववयोगो भवेध्रुवम् ॥ १३ ॥

Stanza 13. For a person born in Aries, Jupiter, in the 11th house cannot give rise to any Yoga during his Dasa.

मेषे जातस्य षष्ठे तु बुधभौमौ स्थितौ यदि ।
तयोर्दशायां संप्राप्तौ व्रणस्फोटादि रोगदौ ॥ १४ ॥

Stanza 14. For one born in Aries, Mercury and Mars in the 6th will give rise to wounds, skin eruptions, small pox and the like during their Dasas.

मेषे जातस्य भौमोऽपि सप्तमे संस्थितः कविः ।
स्वार्जितं भाग्यमाप्नोति किंचिद्धनमुदीरितम् ॥ १५ ॥

Stanza 15. A Person born in Mesha Ascendant will possess self-earned fortune and some wealth also, if Mars and Venus are in the 7th house.

मेषे जातस्य भौमस्तु अष्टमस्थो न योगदः ।
रविशुक्रसमायुक्तः स्वल्पदश्च भविष्यति ॥ १६ ॥

Stanza 16. For one born in Mesha Ascendant Mars in the 8th house does not produce Yoga, he will however confer some fame if he is in conjunction with the Sun and Venus.

भाग्यस्थौ रविभौमौ च गुरूशुक्रौ तथैव च ।
सप्तमस्थो यदि शनिः भौमो योगविशेषदः ॥ १७ ॥

Stanza 17. For a person born in Mesha Ascendant if the Sun and Mars are in the 9th as also Jupiter and Venus, and Saturn is in the 7th then Mars produces special Yoga.

मेषलग्ने तु जातस्य लग्ने रविभृगू यदि ।
गुरूणा वीक्षितौ नोचेत्छुक्रो योगप्रदो भवेत् ॥ १८ ॥

Stanza 18. For a person born in Mesha Ascendant, Venus becomes capable of giving rise to Yoga provided he is in Ascendant with the Sun unaspected by Jupiter.

गुरूणा वीक्षितश्शुक्रौ योगदो न भवेध्रुवम् ।
गुरूणा वीक्षितस्सूर्यो योगदो भवति ध्रुवम् ॥ १९ ॥

Stanza 19. Venus aspected by Jupiter will not certainly confer any Yoga. But the Sun aspected by Jupiter becomes a Yogakaraka.

मेषलग्ने तु जातस्य रविसौम्य सितास्तथा ।
लाभस्था यदि तेषां च दशाभाग्यप्रदा स्मृता ॥ २० ॥

Stanza 20. For a person born in Mesha Ascendant if the Sun, Mercury and Venus are in the 11th, they will give rise to fortune during their respective dasas.

मेषे जातस्य लग्नस्थो भानु कर्कटके यदि ।
चन्द्रो यदि भवेज्जातः राजयोगम् समश्नुते ॥ २१ ॥

Lagna or First House

Stanza 21. For a person born in Mesha Lagna, Raja Yoga is caused if the Sun or Moon is in Cancer.

मेष लग्ने तु जातस्य शुक्रेज्यार्यम्णो यदि ।
राज्यस्थास्तद्दशाकाले गंगास्नानम् भविष्यति ॥ २२ ॥

Stanza 22. A person born in Mesha Jagna will have dips in the Ganges in the dasas of Venus, Jupiter and the Sun if the said planets are in the 10th.

NOTES

The above stanzas are simple enough and do not call for any elaborate explanations. However we may summarise the various principles enunciated therein so that the reader may understand them clearly.

(1) Jupiter in the 11th does not produce any Yoga in his Dasa. (2) Mars and Mercury in the 6th give rise to wounds, skin eruptions, cuts and the like in their dasas (3) Mars cannot produce any Yoga by himself when he is in the 8th in his own house, but can confer slight fame if he is with the Sun and Venus (4) The situation of Venus and Mars in the 7th is favourable for self acquisition of fortune and wealth (5) Mars causes special Yoga when the Sun and Mars and Jupiter and Venus are in Sagittarius and Saturn is in the 7th (6) Venus confers *some fame* if he is in the Ascendant with the Sun unaspected by Jupiter while the Sun confers fame when he receives Jupiter's aspect. (8) The Dasa of the Sun, Mercury and Venus will prove beneficial if the said planets are in the 11th and finally. (9) the Sun in Ascendant and the Moon in Cancer are beneficial as causing Raja Yoga. This particular Yoga appears to have been taken from *Brihat Jataka* (XI. 2).

Chart No. 3—*Born on 9-6-1891 at Gh. 55-20, Lat 19⁰ N., Long. 72⁰ E.*

	Lagna	Venus Sun Rahu Merc.	Mars			Rahu Jupit.	
Jupit.		RASI		Moon	Merc.	NAVAMSA	
				Saturn	Mars Venus		
	Kethu				Lagna	Kethu	Saturn	Sun Moon

Balance of Saturn's Dasa at birth : years 13-10-22

In Chart No. 3 the Moon is in the 4th causing a Raja Yoga Venus is in Ascendant and is unaspected by Jupiter. The native has risen from humble beginnings to a fairly responsible position.

अथ वृषभलग्न विचारः ।
VRISHABHA LAGNA

वृषभजातस्य च शनिः भाग्यकर्मेश्चरोऽपि ।
सूर्यसोमसुताभ्याम् वा न युक्तौ नैव योगदः ॥ १ ॥

Stanza 1. For a person born in Vrishabha Ascendant Saturn does not become Yogakaraka in spite of his owning the 9th and 10th houses from Ascendant, nor do the Sun and Mercury become capable of producing Yoga even if they occupy the Ascendant.

वृषभक्षेऽपि जातस्य राज्येराहुर्यदि स्थितः ।
मकरे गुरूभौमौ वा गंगास्नानम् समश्नुते ॥ २ ॥

Lagna or First House

Stanza 2. A person born in Vrishabha Ascendant will have dips in Ganges if Rahu is in the 10th or Mars and Jupiter are in Capricorn.

वृषभे जायमानस्य चतुर्थे यदि चन्द्रमाः ।
गुरूणा च बुधेनापि वीक्षितो यदि योगदः ॥ ३ ॥

Stanza 3. For one born in Vrishabha Ascendant Moon becomes capable of producing Yoga if he occupies the 4th aspected by Jupiter or Mercury.

वृषभे जायमानस्य कुजस्सप्तमगश्शुभः ।
लाभस्थौ भानुभाग्येशौ दीर्घायुर्योगवान सदा ॥ ४ ॥

Stanza 4. For a person born in Vrishabha Ascendant Mars becomes a benefic in the 7th house Long life is indicated if the Sun and lord of the 9th are in the 11th.

वृषलग्ने तु जातस्य गुरोस्सोमसुतस्य च ।
संबन्धो वीक्षणम् वाऽपि विद्यते धनयोगदः ॥ ५ ॥

Stanza 5. For one born in Vrishabha Ascendant if Jupiter and Mercury are in conjunction or in mutual aspect DhanaYoga is caused.

वृषभे जायमानस्य गुरोस्सोमसुतस्य च ।
कुजेन सहसम्बन्धो वीक्षितो वा भवेद्यदि ।
विशेष धन संग्राप्तिम् न प्राप्नोति न संशयः ॥ ६ ॥

Stanza 6. The DhanaYoga becomes defunct if Jupiter and Mercury are in conjunction with or aspected by Mars.

NOTES

The great Parasara observes thus "RAJA YOGAKARAH SAKSHADEKA YEVA RAVEH SUTHA" meaning that Saturn is the only planet capable of producing Raja Yoga for Taurus Ascendant. In the face of thus ascertain by no less a personage than Parasara the author of the work observes that Saturn even though lord of the 9th and 10th, does not produce Yoga. When two great authors express two different views we have to stick to the opinions of the greater of the two, or rely upon our own experience Parasara is undoubtedly the greatest because he is not only a Maharshi but what he says is held to be beyond question. Our author in suggesting Saturn as incapable of giving good results might have had in view reasons justifiable in their own way and he might not certainly have meant any disrespect for Parasara. When stanza I is clear no other meaning can be read into it than what it implies. Probably the author felt that Saturn, though he many produce Raja Yoga by owning the 9th and 10th houses, might render the native unable to achieve in full measures the fruits of such Yoga because Saturn is by intrinsic nature a malefic. Prof. B. Suryanarayan Rao's words are still ringing fresh in my mind when he said to me that Saturn would doubtless produce Raja Yoga but he would not enable the person to consolidate his gains – political and material. Again much depends upon how Saturn is situated in the horoscope. If he is in the 10th it is a good position. If he is in the 2nd it yields destructive influences. The native earns money, fame and reputation but an outlet for the exit of all these will be present in some form or other.

In stanza 3, Moon is said to be capable of causing Yoga if he occupies the 4th house. But according to Parasara, the Moon is evil for Taurus Ascendant. If the Moon is aspected by Jupiter a Yoga is said to result.

Lagna or First House

Combinations enunciated in stanzas 5 and 6 seem to be sound and reasonable. DhanaYoga is caused by the conjunction of Jupiter and Mercury (lord of 2) and this DhanaYoga becomes defunct if Mars also join the combination. Mars is lord of 12 (house of loss) and naturally wealth indicated will be removed by the 12th lord.

वृषभे जायमानस्य गुरूसौम्यकुज यदि ।
परस्परयुतारस्सौम्यदायस्तु ऋणयोगदः ॥ ७ ॥

Stanza 7. For one born in Taurus Ascendant if Jupiter. Mercury and Mars join together or aspect one another, there will be debts during Mercury's Dasa.

भौमदायस्तु धनदो गुरोर्दायस्तु मिश्रदः ।
केन्द्रस्थितस्य सौम्यस्य दायोर्योगप्रदस्मृतः ॥ ८ ॥

Stanza 8. For a person born in Taurus Ascendant Mars dasa will give financial prosperity and Jupiter dasa produces mixed results; provided Mercury is in a Kendra, he produces Yoga in the course of his Dasa.

लग्नस्थौ बुधशुक्रौ तु सप्तमस्थो गुरूर्यदिः ।
बुधदायस्तु प्रबलयोगदो वृषजन्मनः ॥ ९ ॥

Stanza 9. For one born in Taurus Ascendant, during Mercury Dasa powerful Yoga will be caused, if Mercury and Venus are in the Ascendant and Jupiter is in the 7th.

लग्नस्थौ कुजशुक्रौ तु मकरस्थो गुरूर्यदि ।
गुरूसौम्यदशाकाले भाग्यंस्याद् वृषजन्मनः ॥ १० ॥

Stanza 10. For a person born in Taurus Ascendant if Mars and Venus are in Ascendant, and Jupiter is in Capricorn the Dasas of Mercury and Jupiter will prove fortunate.

मन्दसौम्यकुजा भाग्ये राहुः कुंभगतो यदि ।
कुजराहुदशा गंगास्नानदा वृषजन्मनः ॥ ११ ॥

Stanza 11. A person born in Taurus Ascendant will have dips in Ganges during the Dasas of Mars and Rahu if Saturn Mercury and Mars are in the 9th and Rahu is situated in Aquarius.

चन्द्रशुक्रौ तु षष्ठस्थौ लाभे सौम्यगुरू यदि ।
गुरूदाये च संप्राप्ते धनयोग उदीरितः ॥ १२ ॥

Stanza 12. Jupiter Dasa will cause DhanYoga, if the Moon and Venus are in the 6th and Mercury and Jupiter are in the 11th.

शुक्रस्यदाये संप्राप्ते धनप्रबल्यमादिशेत् ।
भाग्ययोगं समाप्नोति वृषजन्म न संशयः ॥ १३ ॥

Stanza 13. A person born in Taurus Ascendant will undoubtedly get plenty of wealth in the course of Venus Dasa, and he will also enjoy "Bhagya Yoga."

वृषभे जायमानस्य लग्ने चन्द्रस्थितौ यदि ।
विशेष धनयोगं तु न प्राप्नोति जातकः ॥ १४ ॥

Stanza 14. One born in Taurus Ascendant will not have much DhanYoga if the Moon is situated in Ascendant.

इतरर्क्षे जायमानो भाग्यवान् भवित ध्रुवम् ॥ १५ ॥

Stanza 15. If birth happens in other signs (than Taurus) and the Moon is in Ascendant then the native will certainly become fortunate.

NOTES

In these nine stanzas, the formation of Yogas by the different kinds of combinations of planets is

Lagna or First House

discussed. Summarising we may observe that, with reference to Taurus Ascendant—

(1) Mars, Jupiter and Mercury can produce Yoga (confer fame) by mutual combination and aspect. Mercury and Mars may give rise to Yoga as lords of 5th and 7th but how Jupiter being lord of 8th and 11th can form Yoga is incompre hensible. Jupiter can produce fairly good results if he is in the 10th house and not otherwise.

(2) Access to wealth in Mars Dasa mixed result in Jupiter Dasa, and power and fame in Mercury Dasa (if Mercury is in a Kendra) may be predicted.

(3) Good results will be produced in Mercury Dasa if Mercury and Venus are in Ascendant and Jupiter is in the 7th.

(4) Jupiter and Mercury Dasas will be fortunate if Venus and Mars are in Ascendant and Jupiter is in Capricorn.

It will be seen in this combination that Jupiter should be in Capricorn (9th house) where he is debilitated (Neecha). This debilitated effect is said to be cancelled by the disposition of Mars, Mercury and Venus in Ascendant.

(5) There will be access to wealth in Jupiter Dasa if the Moon (lord of 3) and Venus (lord of 6) are in the 6th and Mercury and Jupiter are in the 11th.

(6) The presence of the Moon in Ascendant deprives wealth.

Chart No. 4—*Born on 12-2-1856 at Gh. 12-21, p.m., L.M.T. Lat 80° N., Long. 84° E.*

	Moon Rahu	Ascdt.	Saturn	Jupit.		Ascdt.	Rahu
Sun Merc. Jupit.		RASI				NAVAMSA	
				Merc.			
Venus		Mars Kethu		Kethu		Moon Sun Saturn Venus Mars	

Balance of Venus Dasa at birth : years 6-11-3.

In *Chart No, 4* Jupiter is with Mercury (lord of 2 and 5) and the Sun (lord of 4) in the 10th. The Sun Mercury combination is a distinct Raja Yoga and Jupiter, probably by virtue of his connection with this Raja Yoga derived power to do good is respect of the Bhava occupied by him. The native built up his reputation in the course of Jupiter and had good earning throught out the period. At the end of this Dasa however he fell seriously ill and in the bhukthi of Rahu (mark Rahu is in the 12th ruling feet and aspected by Mars) two fingers in the left foot of the native were removed by a surgical operation. From the Moon, Jupiter is lord of the 9th and is in the 11th and the disposition of planets from the Moon should not be ignored when making predictions.

Lagna or First House

अथ मिथुनलग्न विचारः ।
Mithuna Lagna

तृतीयस्थौ रविबुधौ बुधदाये समागमे ।
बुधो योगप्रदस्सत्यं युग्मजातस्य भाग्यदः ॥ १ ॥

Stanza 1. For a person born in Mithuna (Gemini) Ascendant, if the Sun and Mercury are placed in the 3rd house Mercury will surely produce Yoga in his Dasa besides giving rise to beneficial results.

भृगुभौमेन्दवः खेटा धनस्थाने स्थिता यदि ।
शुक्रदाये धनप्राप्तिं युग्मजातस्समश्नुते ॥ २ ॥

Stanza 2. If Venus Mars and the Moon are in the 2nd during Venus Dasa there will be access to wealth for a person born in Gemini Ascendant.

मिथुने जायमानस्य धरासूनुर्धने स्थितः ।
शनिचन्द्रावष्टमस्थौ शनेर्दाये समागमे ॥ ३ ॥

Stanza 3. For one born in Gemini Ascendant if Mars is in the 2nd and the Moon and Saturn are in the 8th then during the dasa of Saturn:–

शनिस्तु मिश्रफलदः कुजदाये समागमे ।
धनयोगो भवत्येव जातकस्य न संशयः ॥ ४ ॥

Stanza 4. Saturn will give mixed results Mars will undoubtedly give rise to DhanaYoga in his dasa.

मिथुने जायमानस्य कुजमन्दौ द्वितीयगो ।
अष्टमस्थौ भवेदिन्दु शनिभौम दशागमे ॥ ५ ॥

Stanza 5. If Mars and Saturn are in the 2nd and the Moon is in the 8th then when the dasas of Saturn and Mars commence:—

तत्काले धनहीनस्यात्पूर्वभाग्यं विनश्यति ।
किंचिद्धनयुतो जातो भवेदेवं न संशयः ॥ ६ ॥

Stanza 6. The native loses wealth and property will be destroyed but still he will retain some money.

मिथुने जायमानस्य धननाथस्तु चन्द्रमाः ।
मारको न भवत्येव मानवस्य न संशयः ॥ ७ ॥

Stanza 7. The Moon who is the lord of the 2nd does not become a Maraka for a person born in Gemini Ascendant. This is undoubted.

मिथुने जायमानस्य कुजचन्द्रौर् तु लाभगौ ।
भाग्यस्थो यदि वा मन्दो विशेष धनयोगदः ॥ ८ ॥

Stanza 8. A powerful DhanaYoga will be caused for a person born in Gemini Ascendant if the Moon and Mars are in the 11th and Saturn is in the 9th.

युग्मजातस्य भाग्यस्थौ गुरूमन्दौ तयोर्दशा ।
काले भवति गंगायांस्नानं भवति निश्चयः ॥ ९ ॥

Stanza 9. The native will have dips is Ganges and other sacred rivers in the dasas of Jupiter and Saturn provided these planets are in the 9th house.

मिथुन जायमानस्य बुधो लाभस्थितो यदि ।
ज्येष्ठभ्रातृ विरोधस्तु जातकस्य भवेध्रुवम् ॥ १० ॥

Stanza 10. If Mercury is in the 11th house the native will have misunderstandings with his eldest brother.

NOTES

The combinations are clear and can be easily understood by the readers. Mars is a malefic for Gemini Ascendant but according to Stanza 4 one will have access to wealth in Mars Dasa if Mars is

Lagna or First House

in the 2nd and Saturn and the Moon are in the 8th. This means that Mars will be in debilitation and also implies presence of Neechabhanga (by virtue of the Moon lord of 2nd aspecting the 2nd as also Saturn lord of 9th), otherwise Mars cannot give financial prosperity. Stanza 6 makes it clear that if Mars and Saturn are in the 2nd and the Moon is in the 8th wealth will be destroyed in Mars Dasa. The differentiation in disposition for giving wealth and taking away wealth is that for the former result Saturn must be in the 8th with the Moon while Mars should be in the 2nd, and for the latter Moon must be in the 8th while Saturn and Mars must be in the 2nd. The centre of gravity is Saturn. He will destroy the indications of the 2nd if he is present there.

These are indeed unique combinations and call for much power of analysis on the part of the reader to understand their proper implication.

Stanza 8 says that the Moon and Mars in the 11th and Saturn in the 9th give rise to immense wealth.

Chart No. 5—*Born on 11-4-1880 at Gh. 12 after sunrise. Lat 18° N.; Long. 5h. 34m. E.*

Merc. Venus Jupit. Saturn	Moon Sun		Kethu Mars Ascdt.	Kethu Saturn Ascdt.	Sun		
	Chart No. 5 RASI 300—20				NAVAMSA		
							Venus
Rahu				Mars		Jupit. Merc.	Moon Rahu

Balance of Moon's Dasa at birth : years 11-6-27

In Chart No. 5 the Moon is in the 11th. The native rose from ordinary rungs and made a lot of money. The Moon is free from any afflictions and this is a great asset. There are no fewer than 6 planets in the ascendant and the 10th house. This indicates an active and rapidly moving mind fitted to play a mighty part.

अथ कटकलग्न विचार:

Karkataka Lagna

कर्किजातस्य च गुरूर्विशेषेण न योगद: ।
मकरे जायमानस्य बुधो योगप्रदो भवेत् ॥ १ ॥

Stanza 1. Jupiter does not cause any special Yoga for one born in Cancer Ascendant. But Mercury is productive of Yoga for a person born in Capricorn.

कर्कटे जायमानस्य भौमो योगप्रदो भवेत् ।
प चमे वाथराज्येवा योगदो भवति ध्रुवम् ॥ २ ॥

Stanza 2. Mars becomes Yogakara to a person born in Cancer; if he also happens to be either in the 5th or 10th houses, he become more powerful to confer Yoga.

कर्किजातस्य शुक्रस्तु व्ययस्थो धनगोऽपि वा ।
योगप्रदस्तु भवतिह्यन्यत्र नहि योगद: ॥ ३ ॥

Stanza 3. Venus causes Yoga if he is placed either in the 12th or in the 2nd house, in other places he will not produce any Yoga.

कर्किजातस्य भौमेज्य चन्द्राश्च धनगो यदि ।
रविशुक्रौ पचमस्थौ धनवान् भाग्यवान् भवेत् ॥ ४ ॥

Stanza 4. A person born in Cancer Ascendant will become wealthy and fortunate if Mars, Jupiter and

Lagna or First House

the Moon are in the 2nd house and the Sun and Venus are in the 5th house.

बुधशुक्रौ पंचमस्थौ बुधदाये समागमे ।
कर्किंजातस्य च बुधो योगदो भवति ध्रुवम् ॥ ५ ॥

Stanza 5. For a person born in Cancer if Mercury and Venus are in the 5th Mercury will produce Yoga in the course of his dasa.

कर्किंजातस्य लाभे तु सौम्यशुक्रेन्दवस्थिताः ।
लग्नसंस्थो यदि गुरूः राज्यस्थाने स्थितो रविः ॥ ६ ॥

Stanza 6. If Mercury, Venus and the Moon are in the 11th house, Jupiter in the ascendant and Sun in the 10th.

राजाभवेत्साहसिकः गुणवान कीर्तिवान भवेत् ।
बृहज्जातकयोगोयं महाराजिक संज्ञिकः ॥ ७ ॥

Stanza 7. The native will become a king who is capable, famous and of good character. This particular combination goes under the name of MahaRaja Yoga in Brihat Jataka.

NOTES

Jupiter though lord of 9 for Cancer Ascendant will not produce Raja Yoga while Mercury produces Raja Yoga for Capricorn Ascendant. In both these cases, the planets in question own the 6th and 9th houses,— but why should Mercury cause Yoga. The explanation is simple. In respect of Mercury along with the 9th lordship, exaltation place is also combined while this is not the case in reference to Jupiter.

If you examine carefully several horoscopes of person born in Cancer Ascendant you will invariably find that Jupiter in his Dasa has given rise to both good and bad results – bad in respect of debts, diseases and enemies. Though Jupiter may not cause Raja Yoga in the strict sense, he has promoted the business and professional prospects involving the native at the same time in misunderstandings troubles, annoyances and ill-health.

Venus in the 12th or 2nd gives rise to a benefic Yoga. Venus is lord of the 4th and 11th and his presence in the 2nd though in an inimical house is approved by the author.

Chart No. 6—*Born on 29-10-1909 at Gh. 1-15 after sunrise. Lat 13° N.; Long. 77° 34' E.*

Mars	Saturn	Rahu	Sun Merc. Ascdt.
	RASI 300—20		Jupit. Venus
	Moon Kethu		

	Saturn		Venus
Moon	NAVAMSA		Rahu
Kethu			
Ascdt.	Sun	Mars Jupit.	Merc.

Balance of Mercury's Dasa at birth : years 6-6-16

The subject Chart No. 6 is short, strong, nervous, extremely sensitive and dark in complexion. The native is unimaginative, miserly, mean and undignified and cautious. There are several malefic combinations in this horoscope and we are concerned with only two points, viz., Cancer rising as Ascendant and Venus being placed in the 2nd. The native earned fairly decently and also acquired landed properties.

Lagna or First House

रविभौमौ तु राज्यस्थौ धनवान् कर्किजातकः ।
कर्किजातस्य च गुरोर्दशाकालस्तु मारकः ॥ ८ ॥

Stanza 8. A person born in Cancer Ascendant will become rich if the Sun and Mars are in the 10th house. Death will occur in the course of Jupiter Dasa.

कर्कटे जायमानस्य बुधशुक्रौ व्ययस्थितौ ।
शुक्रदाये च संप्राप्ते राजयोग उदीरितः ॥ ९ ॥

Stanza 9. A person born in Cancer Ascendant will enjoy Raja Yoga in the course of Venus Dasa if Mercury and Venus are in the 12th house.

कर्कटे जायमानस्य चन्द्रजीवौ तु लग्नगौ ।
राजयोग इति प्रोक्तःभाग्यवान्कीर्तिमान्भवेत् ॥ १० ॥

Stanza 10. For a person born in Cancer the combination of the Moon and Jupiter in Ascendant results in a Raja Yoga. This makes him fortunate and famous.

कर्कटे जायमानस्य चन्द्रो लग्ने स्थितो यदि ।
मकरस्थो भवेत्भौमः राजयोग उदीरितः ॥ ११ ॥

Stanza 11. Raja Yoga is also caused if the Moon is in Ascendant and Mars is in Capricorn.

कर्कटे जायमानस्य लग्न चन्द्रस्थितो यदि ।
तुलायां यदि मन्दस्तु राजयोग उदीरितः ॥ १२ ॥

Stanza 12. If the moon is in Ascendant and Saturn is in Libra then also Raja Yoga is produced.

कर्कटे जायमानस्य चन्द्रो लग्ने स्थितो यदि ।
मेषस्थितो यदि रविः राजयोग उदीरितः ॥ १३ ॥

Stanza 13. Raja Yoga results if the Moon is in Ascendant and the Sun is in Aries.

कर्किजातस्य लग्नस्थौ रविसौम्यौ तु सौख्यगः ।
कविल्लाभे चन्द्रभौमगुरुः संस्थिता यदि ॥ १४ ॥

Stanza 14. If the Sun and Mercury are in the Ascendant, Venus is in the 4th, and the Moon, Mars and Jupiter are in the 11th.

रवेर्दाये त संप्राप्ते निर्धनं योगमश्नुते ।
इतरेषां दशाकाले योगदास्तु भवन्ति हि ॥ १५ ॥

Stanza 15. The native loses wealth in the course of the Sun's Dasa while in other dasas he will enjoy good results.

गंगास्नानं कर्किजस्य गुरूसौम्यौ तु लाभगौ ।
शनिराहू पंचमस्थौ राहुदाये तु सिध्यति ॥ १६ ॥

Stanza 16. The native will surely have dips in the Ganges in Rahu dasa if Jupiter and Mercury are in the 11th and Saturn and Rahu are in the 5th.

NOTES

These nine stanzas give several Raja Yogas and they need no explanation as the stanzas are quite simple.

अथ सिंहलग्न विचारः

Simha Lagna

सिंहलग्ने तु जातस्य रविसौम्यकुजा यदि ।
परस्परेण संयुक्ता धनबाहुल्यमादिशेत् ॥ १ ॥

Stanza 1. For a person born in Leo Ascendant if the Sun, Mercury and Mars are conjoined together good wealth is indicated.

Lagna or First House

सिंहलग्ने तु जातस्य रविजीवबुधा यदि ।
परस्परेण संयुक्ता धनबाहुल्यमादिशेत् ॥ २ ॥

Stanza 2. If the Sun, Jupiter and Mercury are combined together good wealth is indicated.

सिंहलग्ने तु जातस्य रविसोमसुता यदि ।
अन्योन्य संयुतौ स्यातां स्वल्प भाग्यमुदीरितम् ॥ ३ ॥

Stanza 3. If the Sun and Mercury are in conjunction, the native will enjoy some fortune.

सिंहलग्ने तु जातस्य गुरूशुक्रौ न योगदौ ।
योगभंगकरौ किंतुर्विदुज्ज्योतिषकोत्तमाः ॥ ४ ॥

Stanza 4. The learned in Astrology say that for a person born in Leo Ascendant, Jupiter and Venus do not produce any Yoga. On the other hand they cause destruction of the Yoga.

सिंहलग्ने तुजातरय तृतीयस्थो भृगुश्शुभः ।
राज्यस्थः शुक्रपापस्यान्नयोगं लभते नरः ॥ ५ ॥

Stanza 5. For a person born in Leo Ascendant, Venus becomes a benefic in the 3rd house, he becomes a malefic in the 10th. Therefore Venus can produce no Yoga.

सिंहलग्ने तु जातरय रविसौम्यकुजास्थिताः ।
लग्न बुधदशाकालः धनभाग्यबहुप्रदः ॥ ६ ॥

Stanza 6. The Subject gains much wealth and fortune in Mercury Dasa if the Sun, Mercury and Mars are in the Ascendant.

कुजमन्दौ व्ययस्थौ चेच्छनिदाये समागमे ।
शनियोंगप्रदस्सत्यं सिंहजातस्यवै ध्रुवम् ॥ ७ ॥

Stanza 7. Saturn causes Yoga in his dasa if Mars and Saturn are in the 12th. This is certain.

NOTES

The Sun, Mercury and Mars are said to give rise is wealth if in mutual combination. The Sun is lord of the Ascendant, Mercury lord of wealth and Mars is of course Yogakaraka. Thus all the three planets have acquired some power or other to do good. Jupiter is lord of 5th. Therefore his association is also permissible. If the Sun and Mercury are combined some fortune is granted while Mars stepping in gives immense fortune. As Jupiter and Venus are lords of the 8th and 3rd their combination is not conducive to prosperity. Venus in the 3rd is good while in the 10th he is bad as he owns a Kendra besides being located there. Saturn in the 12th with Mars is good. Thus it will be seen that the Sun, Mercury and Mars play an important role in case of persons born in Leo Ascendant, while other planets will be able to do some good under certain special conditions.

Chart No. 7—*Born on 14-05-1896 at 17 gh. after sunrise. Lat 13° N.; Long. 77° 35' E.*

Mars	Venus	Sun Moon Merc.				Saturn	Ascdt. Kethu
Rahu	Chart No. 7 RASI		Jupit.		NAVAMSA		Moon
			Ascdt. Kethu	Sun			Merc. Mars
		Saturn		Rahu		Jupit.	Venus

Balance of Moon's Dasa at birth: years 2-5-21.

Lagna or First House

In *Chart No. 7* the Sun and Mercury are in the 10th together. The native is earning decently but he has not saved anything.

Chart No. 8—*Born on 28/29.8.1898 at 5-33 a.m. L.M.T. Lat 16° 50' N.; Long. 75° 45' E.*

			Mars Kethu		Moon	Kethu	Jupit.
	Chart No. 8 RASI		Sun Ascdt. Merc.		NAVAMSA		Ascdt.
Moon							Sun
Rahu	Saturn		Jupit. Venus	Merc.	Rahu Mars Saturn		Venus

Balance of Venus Dasa at birth: years 9-8-12.

One the other hand in *Chart No. 8*, the Sun and Mercury are together in a Ascendant and the native is in very well to do circumstances though he had a checkered career.

अथ कन्यालग्न विचार:

Kanya Lagna

कन्यालग्ने तु जातस्य भृगोश्चन्द्रस्य वा यदि ।
संबन्धो यदि विद्यते रवेर्दाये धनागमः ॥ १ ॥

Stanza 1. For person born in Kanya (Virgo) Ascendant if the Sun is related to Venus or the Moon by mutual conjunction, aspect, etc., there will be access to wealth in the course of Sun's Dasa.

NOTES

Here is a combination which suggests that a planet who is the lord of 12th or the house of loss gives access to wealth under certain conditions. As the Sun happens to be the lord of 12th for Virgo he cannot give independent results. He partakes of the results of the planets he is in conjunction with or aspected by. As Venus is lord of the 2nd and the 9th and the Moon is the lord of the 11th, the Sun gives results pertaining to wealth, fortune and gains. It is such combinations which are elusive in their nature and escape the notice of students of Astrology.

शुक्रदाये च संप्राप्ते धनहीनो भवेन्नरः ।
चन्द्रदाये च संप्राप्ते मिश्रायोगं समश्नुते ॥ २ ॥

Stanza 2. The person becomes bereft of wealth in Venus Dasa Mixed results will happen in the course of Moon's Dasa.

NOTES

Here evil results are predicted in the course of Venus Dasa provided Venus is connected with Sun by conjunction or aspect as given in the preceding stanza.

As Venus is the natural enemy of the Sun, and as the Sun becomes beneficial to produce good results, Venus probably becomes deprived of the good results he would have produced pertaining to the 2nd and 9th house if he were not connected with the Sun either by aspect or by conjunction. The evil results ascribed for Venus Dasa should not be predicted if Venus is not subject to conjunction or aspect of the Sun.

Lagna or First House

चन्द्रशुक्रौ सप्तमस्थौ लाभस्थौ यदि वा गुरू ।
मेषे रविर्गुरोर्दाये शुक्रदाये समागमे ॥ ३ ॥

Stanza 3. A person born in Virgo, with the Moon and Venus in the 7th, Jupiter in the 11th and the Sun in Aries will, during the Dasas of Jupiter and Venus:-.

चतुश्र: पचमा जीवकळत्राणि न संशय:।
कन्यायां जायमानस्य राजतुल्यस्य कामिन: ॥ ४ ॥

Stanza 4. Possess 4 or 5 wives who will be alive. And one born in Virgo will also possess women of high rank.

NOTES

There is a difficult combination because it says that a person born in Virgo with the Moon and Venus in the 7th, Jupiter in the 11th and the Sun in Aries, will possess 4 or 5 wives in the course of dasas of Jupiter and Venus. The combination is indeed rare. Three planets are exalted – Venus in the 7th, Sun in the 8th and Jupiter in the 11th. The combination can be adopted to suit modern times and conditions to the extent that a person born with planets disposed as stated above will have a romantic life.

कन्यायां जायमानस्य गुरूशुक्रौ चतुर्थगौ ।
गुरूशुक्रदशाकाले योगदो भवति ध्रुवम् ॥ ५ ॥

Stanza 5. For one born in Virgo, Jupiter and Venus in the 4th produce Yoga in the course of their dasa.

NOTES

Guru or Jupiter happens to be lord of 4th while Venus is lord of 9th. Thus the combination of the lords of the 4th and 9th — a quadrant and a trine respectively, results in Raja Yoga and the planets therefore are empowered to give good results in the course of their dasa and bukthis. In actual practice it is found that Venus Dasa will be more beneficial than that of Jupiter, because Jupiter becomes afflicted, being lord of a Kendra.

कन्यायां जायमानस्य शनिर्लाभस्थितो यदि ।
शनेर्दाये च संप्राप्ते योगयुक्तो भनेन्नरः ॥ ६ ॥

Stanza 6. A person born in Virgo Ascendant will enjoy beneficial results in the course of Saturn's dasa provided Saturn is in the 11th.

अथ तुलालग्न विचारः
Thula Lagna

तुलालग्ने तु जातस्य शनिर्योगप्रदो भवेत् ।
तृतीय षष्ठनाथोऽपि गुरूर्योगप्रदो भवेत् ॥ १ ॥

Stanza 1. For one born in Libra, Saturn produces Yoga. Though lord of the 3rd and 6th Jupiter also becomes capable of producing Yoga.

NOTES

The Saturn becomes Yogakaraka for Libra Ascendant is understandable when we take into account that he owns the 4th and 5th houses Jupiter is lord of the 3rd and 6th and in this particular case he is supposed to produce Yoga for the simple reason that the 3rd and 6th from Libra happen to be upachaya signs and hence beneficial. But the combination is quite against the ordinary rules of astrology which suggest that lords of 3rd, 6th and 11th are always bad.

Lagna or First House

तुलालग्ने तु जातस्य धनसप्तमनायकः ।
न करोति कुजः पापः निधनं तु न संशयः ॥ २ ॥

Stanza 2. For a person born in Libra, though Mars lord of the 2nd and 7th happens to be a malefic, he does not kill the native. There is no doubt about it.

NOTES

Mars become a Maraka and gets death inflicting power because he owns the 2nd and 7th houses. The author seems to opine that in spite of Mars becoming a Maraka he will not kill the native. Why he does not kill is not explained. Mars is a malefic planet and his owning a Kendra neutralizes the evil. This power of neutralizing can at best be interpreted as of some significance in the sense that Mars in the course of his dasa may not cause much harm to the native. But this not mean that he cannot kill him. In a number of horoscopes which we have in our possession there is ample evidence to show that Mars has killed the native. Therefore in the light of actual experience one has to apply this stanza carefully so that the meaning may not be literally interpreted.

तुलायां जायमानस्य गुरूशुक्रौ समन्वितौ ।
अन्योन्यं वीक्षितौ वापि भौममन्देन वीक्षितौ ॥ ३ ॥

Stanza 3. For a person born in Libra if Jupiter and Venus are together, or aspect each other or get themselves aspected by Saturn and Mars:

कुजभानुजसद्गस्थौ गुरोश्शुक्रांतरेपि वा ।
शुक्रदाये गुरोर्भुक्ति कालेस्पोटव्रणादिकौ ॥ ४ ॥

Stanza 4. Or they are in the signs owned by Saturn and Mars, then during Jupiter Dasa, Venus Bhukti or

Venus Dasa Jupiter Bhukthi the native suffers from small-pox, wounds or other similar complaints.

NOTES

These two stanzas are important because they enable the reader to predict what results pertaining to Jupiter are produced during the sub period of Venus, in the major period of Jupiter or *vice versa* under certain given conditions. They are:— (1) Jupiter and Venus should be in conjunction, (2) or they should aspect each other. (3) or they both should be aspected by Saturn and Mars, (4) or they should be situated in the signs owned by Saturn and Mars.

			Jupit. Venus
	Chart No. 9 RASI 29-71		
Mars			
		Ascdt. Saturn	

If any of the above 4 combinations prevail then the person is to suffer from smallpox, wounds and similar other complaints. Here again much care is necessary on the part of the Astrologer to understand the exact significance of the above combinations. In *Chart No. 9* given below Ascendant is Libra, Jupiter and Venus are in the 10th; Saturn is in Ascendnat and Mars is in Capricorn. Thus almost all the conditions comprehended in the above two stanzas are satisfied. Jupiter & Venus are together in one side and both of them are aspected by Saturn and Mars. But yet the native did not suffer from smallpox but had only some wounds and cuts in the course of Jupiter Dasa. In such a typical horoscope a reader will notice that Jupiter is exalted, Mars is exalted and Saturn is exalted. Evidently the malefic influences

Lagna or First House

which are supposed to accrue by a conglo meration of the evil effects are minimized for the simple reason that Jupiter's benefic effects have overpowered those of Mars.

तुलायां जायमानस्य व्ययस्थौ भानुसोमजौ ।
शनिनावीक्षितौस्या तां मध्यायुर्भाग्यवान् पिता ॥ ५ ॥

Stanza 5. For one born in Libra if the Sun and Mercury occupying the 12th are aspected by Saturn the father will be fortunate and will live to middle age.

NOTES

Only one condition should be satisfied and that is both the Sun and Mercury should be in the 12th and they should be aspected by Saturn. The Sun is the Pithrukaraka and naturally his presence in the 12th aspected by Saturn is supposed to reduce the longevity of the father.

तुलालग्ने तु जातस्य रविस्सौरेर्बुधस्य च ।
कुजस्य यदि संबन्धो बहुभाग्यप्रदो भवेत् ॥ ६ ॥

Stanza 6. For a person born in Libra if the Sun, Saturn and Mercury are in any way related to Mars either by combination or by aspect, then Mars becomes capable of producing immense good.

तुलालग्ने तु जातस्य रविस्सौरेर्बुधस्य च ।
कुजस्यवेदुसंबधो राजयोग उदीरितः ॥ 7 ॥

Stanza 7. For one born in Libra if the Sun Saturn and Mercury are combined with Mars or the Moon, Raja Yoga is produced.

NOTES

The above two stanzas reveal that Mars is capable of doing much good if he is combined with Sun, Saturn and Mercury and that Raja Yoga is caused if the same three planets are combined with the Moon or Mars. Here again the respective places in which the combinations occur and the aspects good or bad to which the planets are subject seem to determine the nature and extent of Raja Yoga.

तुलायां जायमानस्तु शुक्रसूर्यबुधा यदि ।
लग्रस्थाः भाग्यवान्जातः धन्वानश्च भवध्रुवम् ॥ ८ ॥

Stanza 8. A person born in the Libra with the Sun Venus and Mercury in Ascendant, becomes fortunate and wealthy.

सौम्यमंदसितादित्याः लग्नस्थाश्चन्द्रभूमिजौ ।
सप्तमस्थो चन्द्रजस्य दशाकाले समागमे ॥ ९ ॥

Stanza 9. If Mercury Saturn and Venus are in Ascendant, or Moon and Mars are in the 7th then in the course of the Dasa of Mercury.

तुलायां चायमानस्तु पुरूषौ धनवान् भवेत् ।
भाग्यवांश्चभवत्ये व संशयो नास्तिवै ध्रुवम् ॥ 10 ॥

Stanza 10. A person born in Libra Ascendant becomes rich and fortunate. There is no doubt about it.

NOTES

The above three stanzas indicate a combination under which one born in Libra can become rich and fortunate and the particular Dasa in which prosperity will be on the Ascendant. When the Sun Venus and

Lagna or First House

Mercury are in Ascendant (Libra) then the Sun is debilitated, Venus is in his own house and Mercury lord of the 9th is in the Ascendant in a friendly house. The situation of Venus in Ascendant (quadrant) cancels the effect of the debilitation of the Sun. Thus when the lord of Ascendant (Venus), lord of the 9th (Mercury), lord of the 11th (the Sun) are together in Ascendant a powerful combination is produced. Added to these if Saturn is also in Ascendant that will be an additional qualification because Saturn a Yogakaraka for Libra Ascendant exalted in the Ascendant fortifies the strength of the Horoscope immensely. The good effects are further supplemented by the Moon and the Mars being in the 7th causing what is called Chandramangala Yoga and hence the entire combination becomes unique in its own way.

अष्टमे तु गुरूर्भाग्ये मन्दोलाभे कुजेन्दुजौ ।
यदि सन्ति तुलाजातः राजयोग विशेषवान् ॥ ११ ॥

Stanza 11. For a person born in Libra a powerful Raja Yoga is caused by the presence of Jupiter in the 8th, Saturn in the 9th and Mars and Mercury in the 11th.

षष्ठे वान्त्ये यदि गुरूर्लग्ने चन्द्रस्थितो भवेत् ।
शनेर्दाये च संप्राप्ते धटजातो हि योगभाक् ॥12॥

Stanza 12. A person born in Libra becomes fortunate during Saturn Dasa provided Jupiter is in the 6th or 12th and the Moon is in Ascendant.

तुलायां जायमानस्या मारको लग्नभार्गवः ।
द्वितीये सप्तमेशोऽपि न भौमो मारको भवेत् ॥ १३ ॥

Stanza 13. For one born in Libra Venus becomes a Maraka if he is in Ascendant. Mars does not become a Maraka even though he is lord of the 2nd and 7th.

NOTES

There was considerable controversy going on in the columns of *The Astrologcial Magazine* whether a planet which become the lord of the Ascendent can also become a Maraka. This was a test question which several readers of *The Astrological Magazine* tried to answer in several ways. In Dr. Tagore's Horoscope according to Vimshottari, Jupiter lord of the Ascendent become a Maraka. Another great writer held the view quoting from Parasara that lord of Ascendent can never become a Maraka. This was controverted, by other well known scholars who in spite of their contention that lord of Ascendent under certain circumstances can become a Maraka quoted in defence of their contention extracts from *Jathaka Chandrika* and views propounded by Prof. B. Suryanarayana Rao in his English Translation of *Jathaka Chandrika*. In our humble opinion it is clear as day light that any planet can become a Maraka irrespective of the fact, he is lord of Ascendent or not. This view is supported by the above stanza when the Author says that Venus becomes a Maraka for people born in Libra Ascendent if he happens to stay in the Ascendent. And this is fully proved in a number of cases.

तुलायां जायमानस्य मन्दो लग्ने स्थितो यदि ।
कर्कटे यदि चन्द्रस्तु राजयोग उदीरितः ॥ १४ ॥

Stanza 14. For one born in Libra, Raja Yoga will be caused if Saturn is in Ascendent and the Moon is in Cancer.

तुलाजातस्य मन्देज्य बुधभौमाः धटे यदि ।
राजस्थ राहुदाये पुण्यतीर्थफलम् तु भवेत् ॥ १५ ॥

Lagna or First House

Stanza 15. A person born in Libra with Saturn, Jupiter, Mercury and Mars in Aquarius and Rahu in the 10th will undertake pilgrimages and have dips in sacred water in the course of Rahu dasa.

अथ वृश्चिकेलग्न विचार:
Vrischika Ascendant

वृश्चिके जायमानस्य गुरूसौम्य परस्परम् ।
संबन्धिनो यदि भवेद्द्विशेष धनयोगदै ॥ १ ॥

Stanza 1. For a person born in Scorpio, if Jupiter and Mercury are in conjunction or in mutual aspect, much wealth will be conferred.

तृतीयस्थौ यदि गुरूरौदार्यमधिकं भवेत् ।
सप्तमस्थास्सूर्यसौम्य शुक्रौ यदि बुधस्य च ॥ २ ॥

Stanza 2. If Jupiter is in the 3rd the native will have a charitable disposition. If the Sun, Mercury and Venus are in the 7th.

दशाकाले तु संप्राप्ते वृश्चिकक्रूषे तु जातक: ।
राजयोगं समाप्नोति महतीं कीर्तिमश्नुते ॥ ३ ॥

Stanza 3. Then during the period (dasa) of Mercury the person will enjoy much fame and power.

गुरूसौम्यौ पचमस्थौ लाभे चन्द्रो भवेद्यदि ।
बहुभाग्य धनोपेत: कीटजन्मा न संशय: ॥ ४ ॥

Stanza 4. A person born in Scorpio Ascendent will undoubtedly become very fortunate and wealthy if Jupiter and Mercury are in the 5th and the Moon is in the 11th.

कीटजातस्य जीवेंधु केतुनो भाग्यगा यदि ।
गुरोर्दशा योगदाही केतोर्दायोव योगद: ॥ ५ ॥

Stanza 5. For a person born in Scorpio Ascendent, if Jupiter, the Moon and Kethu are in the 9th house, fame and power will be conferred during Jupiter Dasa while Kethu Dasa will be ordinary.

NOTES

The author has devoted 22 stanzas for Pisces Ascendent while he has dispensed with Scorpio Ascendant (Vrischika Ascendant) with in a short space.

The combinations given are no doubt valuable. According to Parasara Jupiter is a benefic for Scorpio Ascendent as he is lord of the 2nd and 5th while a combination of the lords of the 9th and 10th (the Moon and the Sun respectively) results in a Raja Yoga. But in this work the author seems to stress on the importance of the mutual conjunction and aspect of Mercury and Jupiter. Mercury is evil as he is lord of the 8th and 11th but he seems to lose the evil nature by being placed in the 7th house with Venus and the Sun (*vide Stanza 2, supra*) to the extent that during his Dasa, Mercury will confer fame and power. The temporary evil of ownership, acquired by Mercury seems to disappear by his presence in Pisces with Jupiter and by the Moon being in Virgo or the 11th. This combination (Stanza 4) may be diagrammatically represented thus as in Chart No. 10.

Jupit. Merc.			
	Chart No. 10		
	Ascdt.		Moon

Lagna or First House

Stanza 4 gives the combination for immense wealth and fortune. Jupiter is the lord of wealth and fortune and he is in the 5th aspected by the Moon lord of the 9th. There is thus Gaja kesari Yoga also which will further fortify the house of wealth.

Mercury though evil (by lordship) happens to be lord of gains and the forces of the 2nd, 5th, 9th and 11th focused on the 5th house give rise to a distinct Dhana Yoga. The principle adumbrated in stanza 5 may be further extended, thus :

(1) The Moon may be in Pisces and Jupiter and Mercury in Virgo.

(2) The Moon may be in Pisces and Jupiter in Cancer and Mercury in Virgo.

(3) The Moon and Mercury may be in Pisces and Jupiter in Cancer.

(4) The Moon and Mercury may be in Pisces and Jupiter in Virgo.

(5) Mercury may be in Virgo, the Moon in Pisces and Jupiter in Cancer.

(6) Mercury may be in Cancer, the Moon in Virgo and Jupiter in Pisces.

Other permutations and combinations may also be obtained similarly.

Stanza 9 comprehends the presence of a very powerful Gajakesari Yoga while the presence of Kethu with the Moon and Jupiter seems to deprive Kethu of the Power of conferring and Yoga during his own Dasa.

अथ धनुर्लग्न विचार:
Dhanur Lagna

धनुर्लग्ने तु जातस्य पचमस्थ शनेर्दशा ।
शुभप्रदायोगदेति वदन्ति विभुदोत्तमाः ॥ १ ॥

Stanza 1. For a person born in Sagittarius Saturn produces good results and confers Yoga in his Dasa, if he is in the 5th house.

धनुर्लग्ने तु जातस्य लाभस्थो योगदश्शनिः ।
इतरक्षे तु जातस्य लाभमन्दो न योगदः ॥ २ ॥

Stanza 2. For a person born in Sagittarius (Dhanus), Saturn in the 11th confers Yoga; for a person born in other Ascendants, Saturn in the 11th does not cause any Yoga.

धनुर्जस्य भृगु रवि भाग्ये मन्दस्तृतीयगः ।
शनिर्दाये तु भवतो भाग्ययोग धनागमौ ॥ ३ ॥

Stanza 3. A person born in Sagittarius, with the Sun and Venus in the 9th and Saturn in the 3rd will enjoy fame and wealth in the course of Saturn (Sani) Dasa.

कुंभे भौम रवि राहु सिंहगो यदि तद्दशा ।
कालेद्युसरितस्नम् धनुर्जातस्समश्नुते ॥ ४ ॥

Stanza 4. A person born in Sagittarius with Mars and the Sun in Aquarius (Kumbha) and Rahu in Leo will have a bath in the sea in Rahu Dasa.

NOTES

A careful reading into the above stanzas seems to bring out one important fact, viz., the lord of the 11th (who is generally declared evil) produces good results

Lagna or First House

if he is in conjunction with a trinal lord or quadrangular lord (who is a natural malefic). For example on page 39 stanzas 1 while dealing with Scorpio Ascendant (Vrischika Ascendant) the author seems to imply that Dhana Yoga is caused by the conjunction or mutual aspect of Jupieter and Mercury Jupiter is no doubt a natural benefic. But for Scorpio Ascendant be becomes a trinal lord (other konadhipathi) while Mercury is lord of 8th and 11th. Again in stanza 2 under Scorpio Ascendant, Mercury (Budha) dasa is said to confer Raja Yoga if Mercury is in the 7th with Venus and the Sun Venus as *Kendradhipathi* be comes evil while the Sun alone is a (temporary) benefic as owning the 10th.

Again in stanza 3 under Sagittarius Ascendant (Dhanur Lagna) the author makes it clear that Saturn produces good in his Dasa if he is in Aquarius (Khumbh) and the Sun and Venus are in 9th or Leo (Simha). Venus is lord of 11th for Sagittarius Ascendent and his association with the Sun means association with a trinal lord. Unless Venus loses (some of) the evil effects of his 11th house lordship, his aspect over Saturn cannot be construed as so good as to enable Saturn to confer wealth and fame in his Dasa Saturn and Sun are bitter enemies the Sun and Venus are bitter enemies. Only Saturn and Venus are friends. The conjunction of the Sun (9th lord) and Venus (11th lord) in the 9th – like poles being brought together –seems to repel each other's bad qualities and rendering the aspect of Venus favourable. I may not be quite correct in my explanations. But this is how I understand the principle and I am open to conviction. The author gives peculiar combinations and as far as my humble experience goes most of them seem to satisfy practical application.

अथ मकरलग्न विचार:
Makara Lagna

मकरे जायमानस्य अष्टमस्थो भवेद्बुध: ।
लग्नसंस्थो यदि गुरू शुक्रेण च निरीक्षित: ॥ १ ॥

Stanza 1. For a person born in Capricorn Ascendant (Makar Lagna) if Mercury is in the 8th and Jupiter is in Ascendent aspected by Venus.

दीर्घायुर्योगमाप्नोति जातस्तत्र न संशय: ।
निर्धनश्च भवेज्जातोह्वात्रापि च न संशय: ॥ २ ॥

Stanza 2. Long life will no doubt be conferred, but poverty will also be undoubtedly caused.

मकरे जायमानस्य पंचमस्थेदूभृगुश्शुभ: ।
राज्यस्थश्चेदभृगुर्योगं न ददाति कदाचन् ॥ ३ ॥

Stanza 3. For a person born in Capricorn Venus in the 5th house is good, if however he is in the 10th, he may not give rise to any Yoga.

मकरे जायमानस्य लग्नस्थौ शुक्रचन्द्रजौ ।
पंचमस्थश्च चन्द्रस्तु गुरूणा वीक्षितो यदि ॥ ४ ॥

Stanza 4. One born in Capricorn with Venus and Mercury in Ascendent and the Moon in the 5th aspected by Jupiter.

मंडलाधीश्वरो राज भवध्येव न संशय: ।
भृहज्जातकयोगोऽयं महाराजक संज्ञिक: ॥ ५ ॥

Stanza 5. Will undoubtedly become an emperor. This Yoga is termed as Maharaja Yoga according to *Brihat Jataka*.

Lagna or First House

लग्नसंस्थो यदि गुरूर्लाभे शुक्र कुजो यदि ।
गुरूदांये तु संप्राप्ते भ्रातृ मूल धनागमः ॥ ६ ॥

Stanza 6. If Jupiter is in Ascendent and Venus and Mars are n the 11th, the native will get money through brothers in the course of Jupiter (Guru) Dasa.

अन्दोलिका वाहनां च मकरे जातको नरः ।
लभते मात्र सन्देहस्सूरिभिः परिकीर्तितः ॥ ७ ॥

Stanza 7. The learned in Astrology have said that a person born in Capricorn Ascendant (Makar Lagna) will get access to palanquins and other conveyances.

रविचन्द्र बुधालग्ने व्ययो शुक्र कुजा यदि ।
भ्रातृभाग्यम् स्वभाग्यं च प्राप्नोति मृगजो नरः॥ ८ ॥

Stanza 8. If the Sun, the Moon and Mercury are in Ascendant and Mars and Venus are in the 12th, the native will not only get wealth from brothers but will also earn himself.

मृगजन्मा मन्दसौम्य भाग्यस्थौ भाग्यवान् भवेत् ।
व्ययस्थो राहु जीवौ तु राहुर्योगप्रदो भवेत् ॥ ९ ॥

Stanza 9. For a person born in Capricorn (Makara), Saturn and Mercury in the 9th confer fortune. Rahu becomes Yoga karaka if he is in the 12th with Jupiter (Guru).

मकरे जायमानस्य चन्द्रः कर्कट के स्थितः ।
मकरस्थ धरासूनु राजयोगप्रदो भवेत् ॥ १० ॥

Stanza 10. For a person born in Capricorn Ascendant Raja Yoga is caused by the presence of the Moon in Cancer and Mars in Capricorn.

NOTES

The stanzas are clear enough and need no further explanations. However some of the statements are vague and leave the reader where he is without making him understand the principles clearly. The 1st and 2nd stanzas suggest that Mercury no doubt bestows longevity if he is in the 8th but the native will suffer from poverty. This is quite consistent. Because he is lord of the 9th or fortune he will be occupying the 12th or house of loss (from the 9th) if he is in the 8th from Ascendent thus causing loss of fortune.

Venus is the Yogakaraka for Capricorn Ascendant. Whilst he will produce good results in the 5th his presence in the 10th is not approved. For Capricorn Venus not only owns a trine (Taurus) but also a quadrant. When he is in the 5th it is good because as lord of a trine he will be in a trine. He also owns a quadrant (Libra) and this is bad for a benefic. Coupled with this if he also occupies a quadrant he will be powerless to produce any Raja yoga. Quadrangular ownership (Kendradhipathya for benefies and that too for Jupiter and Venus) is held to be productive of extremely bad results Stanzas 6 hints at a distinct Neechabhanga Raja Yoga with particular reference to Capricorn. If Jupiter is in Ascendant, he is Neecha. But if Venus a Yogakaraka for Capricorn is in the 11th with Mars (the planet who gets exalted in Capricorn) the debilitation effect is cancelled with the result that Jupiter gives money through brothers (because Mars responsible for cancellation of Neecha is lord of brothers and Jupiter is lord of the house of brothers) Stanza 7 is vague because every one born in Capricorn Ascendent cannot aspire to possess palanquins and conveyances.

Lagna or First House 47

The Raja Yoga implied in stanza 9 by the conjunction of Saturn (lord of Ascendant) and Mercury (lord of 9) in the 9th is understandable even according to ordinary canons of astrology.

अथ कुम्भलग्न विचारः
Kumbha Lagna

कुंभे सिंहे तु जातस्य योगो नैव विशेषकः ।
भाग्यराज्येश सम्बन्धमात्रेणेति विदुर्भुधाः ॥ १ ॥

Stanza 1. The learned in Astrology have said that for persons born in Aquarius and Leo Ascendant no particular Yoga is caused by the mere combination of the lords of the 9th and 10th.

लग्ने शुक्रविराज्ये राहुर्वा कुंभसद्मनः ।
गुरूराहुदशाकाले योगदो भवतो ध्रुवम् ॥ २ ॥

Stanza 2. For a person born in Aquarius, if Venus is in Ascendant, the Sun is in the 10th and Rahu is in Aquarius Yoga will be caused in the Dasas of Rahu and Jupiter.

Stanza 3. For a person born in Acquarius if the Sun and Mars are in the 8th sorrow will be caused in their Dasas. But during Mercury dasa good will result.

कुंभे तु जायमानस्य रन्ध्रस्थौ रविभूमिजौ ।
तयोर्दाये दुःखदस्या बुधदाये हि योगदः ॥ ३ ॥

Stanza 4. For a person born in Aquarius, if Jupiter is in Ascendant and Saturn is in the 2nd. Mixed results will be produced in Jupiter Dasa and no good will be produced in Saturn Dasa.

घटजातस्य लग्नस्थो गुरूर्मंदो द्वितीयग: ।
गुरूदाये मिश्रयोग: शनिदायेव योगद: ॥ ४ ॥

Stanza 5. Venus gives rise to Yoga in his Dasa if Saturn and Venus are in the 11th house.

कुंभे तु जायमानस्य शनि शुक्रो तु लाभगौ ।
शुक्रदाये च संप्राप्ते शुक्रो भवति योगद: ॥ ५ ॥

Stanza 6. For a person born in Aquarius if the Sun, Mercury and Jupiter are in the 3rd, the Sun becomes beneficial and capable of conferring political power.

NOTES

The author has stressed on the negative value of the association of lords of 9 and 10 in producing Raja Yoga, e.g., Mars (Kuja's) ownership of the 10th devoid of corresponding owner ship of a trinal house. We have to humbly differ from the author's view because the combination of the lords of the 9th and 10th has been found to produce quite auspicious results in actual practice. Moreover, the author of *Jatakachandrika* inclines to the view that combination of Venus and Mars produces Raja Yoga (*vide Jatakachandrika*) English translation by Prof. B. Surayanaryan Rao).

Parasara has cleary stated in his *Brihat Parasara Hora* that Venus alone is a benefic for Aquarius (Kumbh) Ascendant *Daitya Guruh Shubhah* and he further says that Mars produces Raja Yoga. We do not know what prompted the author of this book to observe that the mere combinations of the lords of 9th and 10th does not produce any good. Probably he implies that the combination to be productive of good should occur, in certain beneficial houses.

Lagna or First House

The Parivarthana Yoga implied in stanza 4 about Jupiter being in the Ascendant and Saturn being in the 2nd deserves our careful attention. Instead of Saturn being in the 2nd if he aspects the 2nd house – and Jupiter is in Ascendant even Saturn Dasa will produce quite beneficial results. If however the 2nd house is aspected by Jupiter and the Ascendant is aspected by Saturn – both the Dasas of Jupiter and the Saturn will produce beneficial results building up the career of the native.

Chart No. 11—*Born on 27/28-5-1903 at 1 – 19 a.m. Lat. 9° N.; Long 77° 42' E.*

Kethu	Sun Moon Merc. (R)	Venus	Mars		Sun Venus	Saturn Ascdt. Jupit.
Ascdt. Jupit.	RASI				NAVAMSA	Rahu
Saturn (R)			Kethu			Moon Merc.
		Mars Rahu				

Balance of Mercury's Dasa at birth : years 5-4-24.

In Chart No. 11, Jupiter is in Ascendant while Saturn Lagnadhipathi, instead of being placed in Pisces, aspects Pisces from his own sign Capricorn. The dignity of a planet in any given combination should always be judged after a careful consideration of its disposition both in the Rasi and Navamsa. From the Moon Saturn owns the 9th and 10th houses and aspects the 2nd house. Hence the Dasa Saturn will be conducive for financial prosperity.

In Chart No. 12 Jupiter aspects the 2nd Saturn aspects Ascendant — each Bhava being aspected by its own lord. This combination is quite conducive for the financial prosperity of the native during both the Dasas of Jupiter and Saturn.

Chart No. 12—*Born on 8-8-1912 at about 7-23 p.m. L.M.T. Lat 13° N.; Long 5h. 10m. 20s. E.*

Rahu	Moon Saturn			Saturn	Venus
Ascdt.	RASI	Sun	Rahu Sun	NAVAMSA	Kethu Moon Merc.
		Mars Merc. Venus	Ascdt.		
	Jupit.	Kethu		Jupit.	Mars

Balance of Mercury's Dasa at birth : years 6-0-10.

अथ मीनलग्न विचार:
Meena Lagna

मीने कुम्भे च जातस्य व्ययशुक्रो न योगद: ।
इतरे जायमानस्य व्ययशुक्रशुभप्रद: ॥ १ ॥

Stanza 1. For a person born in Pisces (Meena) or Aquarius (Kumbha) Venus in the 12th does not give rise to any Yoga. For a person born in other Ascendant Venus in the 12h produces benefic results.

मीनलग्ने तु जातस्य व्ययमन्दो हि योगद: ।
लग्नात् व्यये स्थितश्चन्द्रो धनहीनो भवेन्नर: ॥ २ ॥

Stanza 2. For person born in Pisces Ascendant,

Lagna or First House

Saturn in the 12th is good. The native becomes bereft of wealth if the Moon is in the 12th.

मीनलग्ने तु जातस्य गुरोदांये समागमे ।
चन्द्रान्तर्भुक्तिकालस्तु पूर्वयोगस्वहुसृदः ॥ ३ ॥

Stanza 3. For a person born in Pisces, the Yoga referred to earlier becomes reduced in the sub-period of Moon in the Dasa of Jupiter.

NOTES

The only Yoga referred to above is the presence of Saturn in the 12th Stanza 3 reads that the Yoga becomes ineffective or reduced in Jupiter Dasa, Moon's Bukthi. In other words for a person born in Pisces, Saturn's situation in the 12th or Aquarius results in a Yoga and the indications of this Yoga gets reduced in the course of Jupiter Dasa, Moon Bukthi Stanza 3 is not at all clear because it has not explained how the Yoga generated as per stanza 2 could get obstructed in the Dasa of Jupiter within the Bhukthi of Moon.

Chart No. 13—*Born on 24-3-1883 at 6 a.m. (L.M.T.) Lat 13° N.; Long 77° 35' E.*

	Rasi				Navamsa		
Sun Ascdt.	Kethu	Saturn	Jupit.	Mars	Merc. Rahu	Moon	
Mars Merc.	Chart No. 13 RASI				NAVAMSA		
Venus	HJH-39			Saturn			
	Rahu	Moon		Ascdt. Sun Jupit. Kethu	Venus		

Balance of Moon's Dasa at birth : years 5-11-16.

In the above horoscope (Ch No. 13) Saturn aspect the 12th. Let us assume that some Yoga is caused. In Jupiter Dasa Moon's Bukthi the native lost his eye sight and became completely dependent upon others. What Connection these particular directions had with Saturn and the loss of eyesight, intelligent readers must anticipate. Stanzas 2 and 3 may be interpreted to mean that if Saturn is in the 12th house or aspects the 12th then during the Moon's sub-period in the Dasa of Jupiter the person will suffer from sorrows troubles, loss of organs and other misfortunes.

मीनलग्ने तु जातस्य पचमस्थो गुरूर्यदि ।
स्त्रीसन्तति समृद्धिस्यात् कुत्रचित्पुत्र सन्ततिः ॥ ४ ॥

Stanza 4. A person born in Pisces Ascendant with Jupiter in the 5th will have more daughters and few sons.

मीनलग्ने तु जातस्य द्वितीये यदि चन्द्रमाः ।
पचमस्थो यदि कुजश्चन्द्रदाये धनागमः ॥ ५ ॥

Stanza 5. The person will have access to wealth in Moon Dasa if the Moon is in the 2nd and Mars is in the 5th.

मीने तु जायमानस्य गुरूषष्ठेऽष्टमे भृगुः ।
भाग्ये शनिश्चन्द्रकुजौ लाभेचोत्कृष्टभाग्यवान्ः ॥ ६ ॥

Stanza 6. The person will become highly fortunate if Jupiter is in the 6th, Venus in the 8th Saturn is in the 9th, and Mars and the Moon are in the 11th.

मीने तु जायमानस्य चन्द्रसौम्यकुजा यदि ।
मकरस्था यदि भवन् धन वाहन योगदाः ॥ ७ ॥

Stanza 7. A person born in Pisces will possess wealth and vehicles if the Moon, Mercury and Mars are in Capricorn.

Lagna or First House

मीने जातस्य लग्नस्थो शनिचन्द्रौ च लाभगः ।
फुजष्षष्ठेकविश्शुक्रदाये भाग्यमुदीरितम् ॥ ८ ॥

Stanza 8. Predict fortune in Venus Dasa for one born in Pisces Ascendant if Saturn and the Moon are in Ascendant, Mars in the 11th and Venus is in the 6th.

मीने तु जायमानस्य सोम्यजीवेन्दु भूमिजाः ।
चतुर्थस्था यदि भवन् शुक्रेण रहिता यदि ॥ ९ ॥

Stanza 9. For a person born in Pisces, if Mercury, Jupiter, the Moon and Mars except Venus are in the 4th house.

तद्दशान्तर्दशाकाले कीर्तिमाप्नोति शाश्वतम् ।
सिंहासनस्थो भवति राजराजो भवेन्नरः ॥ १० ॥

Stanza 10. Then in the course of the Dasas of these planets (except Venus) he will be become crowned as king and will enjoy much fame.

मीनजातस्य पुंसस्तु लग्नराज्याधिपो गुरूः ।
राज्ये स्थितो यदि भवेद्योगदश्च भवे ध्रुवम्ः ॥ ११ ॥

Stanza 11. For a person person born in Pisces Raja Yoga is certainly caused if the lord of Ascendant and 10th viz Jupiter occupies the 10th.

मीनजातस्य वृषभे चेन्दुसिंसहे रविर्यदि ।
कन्यायां सोमपुत्रस्तु धटे शुक्रो धनुगुरूः ॥ १२ ॥

Stanza 12. For a person born in Pisces, the Moon in Taurus, the Sun in Leo, Mercury in Virgo Venus in Libra and Jupiter in Sagittarius.

कुम्भे शनिः कुजोलाभे बहुभाग्यमुदीरितम् ।
एकद्विखचराभ्यां वा हीनोपूर्वक्रुष संगमः ॥ १३ ॥

Stanza 13. Saturn in Aquarus and Mars in the 11th give rise to much fortune. If one or two combinations as per previous stanza are not present.

भाग्यवान् गुणवान्श्चेव महतीं कीर्तिमश्नुते ।
बृहज्जातकयोगोऽयम् विद्बुद्धिः परिकीर्तितः ॥ १४ ॥

Stanza 14. The person becomes not only fortunate and of good character but will also get immense fame. This Yoga is BrihtajathakaYoga.

NOTES

All the stanzas are clear excepting the last three which mean that for a person born in Pisces, a great Yoga will be crused by the presence of the Sun Mercury, Venus Jupiter and Saturn in their own houses, and the Moon and Mars in their exaltation houses Stanza 13 says that if out of the above one or two dispositions the Sun in Leo and the Moon in Taurus or Mars in Capricorn and Mercury in Virgo and so on, are not present even then, the full effects of the Yoga will be conferred.

Thus ends the First Chapter entitled Ascendant Yoga in *Bhavartha Ratnakara* of Sri Ramanujacharya.

Chapter 2

अथ धनयोग विचार:
Dhana Yogas

धनेशे पचमस्थे च पचमेशो धने यदि ।
धनपे लाभगे वापि लाभेशो धनगो यदि ॥ १ ॥

Stanza 1. If the lord of the 2nd is in the 5th and the lord of the 5th is in the 2nd or if the lord of the 2nd is in the 11th and the lord of the 11th is in the 2nd.

पचमेशो पंचमे वा भाग्ये भाग्याधिपो यदि ।
विशेष धन योगश्चेत्याहुर्जातकको विदः ॥ २ ॥

Stanza 2. If the lord of the 5th is in the 5th and the lord of the 9th is in the 9th the learned in astrology say that much wealth will be earned.

धनलाभाधि पत्योर्हिंधनयोगम् नवै बिना ।
नव पचमेशयोरन्यरेण सहसंगति ॥ ३ ॥

Stanza 3. Dhana Yoga will result if the lords of the 2nd and 11th are combined with lords of the 5th and 9th. If such 2nd and 11th lords are conjoined by other lords (than 5th and 9th) no Dhana Yoga will be formed.

विशेष धनयोगस्य चाभावे व्यस्तिस्वल्पकम् ।
इति दैवज्ञमणयो वदंति विभुदोत्तमाः ॥ ४ ॥

Stanza 4. Though immense wealth may not result the native will earn some wealth. Thus opine the learned in astrology.

Chart No. 14—*Born on 23-10-1898 at 11-30 p.m. (L.M.T.); Lat 19° 10' N.; Long 75° E.*

			Kethu		Kethu		
	Chart No. 14 RASI		Mars Ascdt.		NAVAMSA		
Moon				Venus Merc.			Mars
Rahu	Venus Saturn	Sun Merc. Jupit.		Sun Saturn		Jupit. Rahu	Ascdt. Moon

Balance of Mars' Dasa at birth : years 4-9-29.

NOTES

Stanzas 1 to 3 are clear enough Stanza 4 means that if the lord of the 2nd and 11th are combined with other lords than those of the 5th and 9th the Dhana Yoga referred to in Stanza 3 will not manifest itself in full but there will be access to wealth on a humble scale. The majority of horoscopes belong to this category.

In Chart No. 14 lord of the 2nd Sun is aspected by Mars lord of the 5th Lord of the 2nd is also in conjunction with the lord of the 9th Jupiter. There have given rise to much wealth.

धन लाभाधिपत्योश्च व्ययेशेन सहस्थितिः ।
सबधो यदि विधेत धनाधिक्यं न विद्यते ॥ ५ ॥

Stanza 5. Much wealth will not be acquired if the lords of the 2nd and 11th are combined with lord of the 12th.

Dhana Yogas

Chart No. 15—*Born on 14-5-1896 at 17-0 Gh. at Lat 13° 10' N.; Long 77° 35' E.*

Mars	Venus	Sun Moon Merc.				Saturn	Ascdt. Kethu
Rahu	Chart No. 15 RASI		Jupit.		NAVAMSA		Moon
			Kethu Ascdt.	Sun			Mars Merc.
		Saturn		Rahu		Jupit.	Venus

Balance of Moon's Dasa at birth : years 2-5-21.

NOTES

In *Chart No. 15* Mercury lord of the 2nd and 11th is with Moon lord of the 12th. The native possesses ordinary wealth. There are several afflictions in this horoscope especially the Dwirdwadasa positions of planets.

गुरोश्च धनकारस्य धनाधिपतिना सहा ।
संबन्धश्च बुधेनापि धनयोग उदीरितः ॥ ६ ॥

Stanza 6. Dhana Yoga is found if Jupiter is conjoined with the lord of the 2nd and Mercury.

लाभेशो लाभगोवाऽपि लग्नेशो लग्नगो यदि ।
धनेशो धनगश्चैव धनयोग इतीरितः ॥ ७ ॥

Stanza 7. Dhana Yoga is also caused if lords of the 11th the 1st and the 2nd are in their respective houses.

धनेशो लाभराशीशः उभौ लग्नगतौ यदि ।
धनयोग इति प्रोक्तः बुधैर्जातककोविदैः ॥ ८ ॥

Stanza 8. Learned astrologers say that Dhana Yoga would result of both the lords of the 2nd and 11th are in Ascendant.

NOTES

Three more combinations are given in stanzas 6 7 and 8 for the acquisition of money, viz., (a) the 11th, 2nd and 1st lords should be in their respective houses (b) Jupiter must be combined with lord of the 2nd and Mercury and (c) lords of the 2nd and 11th should be in Ascendant. Combinations are simple enough to understand. In this horoscope (*Chart No. 16*) Jupiter himself is lord of the 2nd and he is in a Kendra. Jupiter is also lord of the 11th and aspects Ascendant. These two combinations are indicative of much wealth especially in Jupiter Dasa.

Chart No. 16—*Born on 8-8-1912 at about 7-23 p.m. (L.M.T.) at Lat 13° N.; 77° 35' E.*

Rahu	Saturn Moon				Saturn	Venus
Ascdt.	Chart No. 16 RASI	Sun	Sun Rahu	NAVAMSA		Kethu Moon Merc.
		Mars Merc. Venus	Ascdt.			
	Jupit.		Kethu		Juipit.	Mars

Balance of Mar's Dasa at birth : years 6-0-10.

In the horoscope (*Chart No. 17*) lord of the 2nd and 11th is Mercury and he is in Ascendant, a very good combination for wealth. The native has earned considerably and is well off financially

Dhana Yogas

Chart No. 17—*Born on 28/29-8-1898 at 5-33 a.m. (L.M.T.) at Lat 61° 50' N.; Long. 5h. 3m. E.*

			Mars Kethu		Moon	Kethu	Jupit.
	Chart No. 17 RASI		Sun Ascdt. Merc.		NAVAMSA		Ascdt.
Moon							Sun
Rahu	Saturn		Jupit. Venus	Merc.	Mars Saturn Rahu		Venus

Balance of Moon's Dasa at birth : years 9-8-12.

सर्वेषु भावस्थानेषु तत्तद्भावादिकारकः ।
विद्यते तस्यभावस्य फलम् स्वल्पमुदीरितम् ॥ ९ ॥

Stanza 9. If the different Karakas are present in their respective bhavas, such bhavas lose vitality and give rise to very little of their indications.

NOTES

This is an important stanza. It says that bhavas will be destroyed if they are occupied by their respective Karakas. The Sun is *Pitrukaraka*, the indicator of father, the Moon—indicator of mother (*Mathrukaraka*); Mars—brothers, Mercury—Karma or profession, Jupiter—children. Venus—wife, Saturn-longevity. Rahu—maternal relations and Kethu paternal relations. The ninth house rules father and the Sun is the Karaka of father. If the Sun is in the 9th then, the 9th bhava becomes afflicted Mars in the third affects the brothers and so on. Saturn seems to be an exception as also Jupiter. If Saturn—the Karaka for longevity is in the 8th—the house of longevity, then instead of reducing the longevity Saturn confers long life. Similarly if Jupiter, Karaka for wealth is in the 2nd, then the 2nd house indications are promoted. These are exceptions to the general rule.

सप्तमाधिपतिश्चन्द्रो धनस्थाने स्थितो यदि ।
केवलेन्दुश्च धनगो नष्टद्रव्यागमो भवेत् ॥ १० ॥

Stanza 10. If the Moon happening to be the lord of the 7th is in the 2nd, alone, the native gets back his lost wealth.

NOTES

This is possible only in case of Capricorn Ascendant horoscopes. Here the author emphasizes that the very presence of Moon in the 2nd secures for the native, lost wealth if any. When the 7th lord is in the 2nd it is clear that the person gets money through the 7th house indications such as marriage and business partners.

Chart No. 18—*Born on 16-10-1981 at 2-26 p.m. (I.S.T.) at Lat 13° N.; Long. 77° 35'. E.*

		Kethu	Jupit.			Saturn Jupit.	
Moon	Chart No. 18 RASI			Rahu	NAVAMSA		Venus
Ascdt.			Saturn	Moon			Kethu
	Rahu	Merc. Sun	Venus	Mars		Merc. Sun	Ascdt.

Balance of Rahu's Dasa at birth : years 11-8-20.

In Chart No. 18 the Moon lord of the 7th is in the 2nd. The native has not lost any wealth. But after the marriage the financial circumstances have improved considerably. Note also the presence of Saturn, Ayushkaraka in the 8th or Ayushthana suggesting long life. The author has not referred to modifications of results in the above combination if the Moon is aspected and otherwise conjoined. However, it is understood that aspectal and conjunctional peculiarities have a modifying or qualifying influence.

अथ निर्धनयोग विचार:
Nirdhana Yogas
Combinations for Poverty

लग्नवाहन भाग्येशाह्वाष्टमस्थान संस्थिता: ।
जातो जननमारभ्य महद्दारिद्रमश्नुते ॥ १ ॥

Stanza 1. If the lords of the Ascendant, the 4th and the 9th are in the 8th the person suffers poverty from his very birth.

धनेशे व्ययभावस्थे व्ययेशो धनगो यदि ।
जातस्य निर्धनो योगो वक्तव्यस्थ सदा बुधै ॥ २ ॥

Stanza 2. If the lord of the 2nd is an the 12th and the lord of the 12th is in the 2nd the native always suffer poverty.

धनेशो व्ययराशोस्यात् व्ययेशे लग्नगे यदि ।
मारकग्रहसंदृष्टौ निर्धनश्च भवेन्नर: ॥ ३ ॥

Stanza 3. A person becomes bereft of wealth if the lord of the 2nd is in the 12th and the lord of the 12th is in Ascendant aspected by a maraka planet.

पंचमेशो रिपुस्थश्चेद्भाग्येशो रन्ध्रगो यदि ।
मारकग्रह संदृष्टौ निर्धनश्च भवेन्नर ॥ ४ ॥

Stanza 4. Poversty is indicated if the lord of the 5th is in the 6th and the lord of the 9th is in the 8th aspected by a maraka planet.

NOTES

The author now gives four combinations for poverty. A careful consideration of these combinations suggests that poverty will result by certain malefic depositions of the lords of the Ascendant the 2nd the 5th and the 9th. Whatever may be the nature of combinations causing poverty or wealth the strong and powerful disposition of Ascendant and its lord will exercise a powerful influence in maintaining the *status quo* of the native in the difference spheres of his activities. The combinations for poverty mentioned in the above stanzas,

(1) Lords of the Ascendant, 4th and 9th should be in the 8th. If all the above three lords are in the 8th that native will be very poor. By implication it is meant that if one or two of the above lords are in the 8th the degree of poverty is lessened. There is a lot of difference between a person who is very poor and starving and one who is moderately poor and can afford at least of the necessities of life Prof. B. Suranarayana Rao has dealt with the combinations in a masterly way in his book *Sarwartha Chintamani* and the reader will do well to refer to the English Translation of this famous book.

(2) There must be parivarthana or exchange of places between the 2nd and 12th lords. If the 2nd lord is in the 12th and the 12th lord is in the 2nd, extreme poverty will result, If the 2nd lord is in the 12th but the latter is not in the 2nd. And if the 12th lord is in the 2nd

Dhana Yogas

but the latter is not in the 12th the degree of poverty will vary. These niceties should be carefully noted in making predictions as otherwise one is bound to hit off the mark in his conclusions.

(3) The third combination suggests that poverty is caused by the lord of wealth being in the 12th and the 12th lord being in Ascendant aspected by a Maraka.

This means that if the Maraka does not aspect the lord of 12th in 1st, then poverty should not be predicted.

(4) The lord of the 5th in the 6th and the lord of the 9th in the 8th aspected by a Maraka will also result in poverty. If the combination is devoid of the aspect of a Maraka though much poverty may not result the native will have to struggle and he will not have a smooth financial career. Poverty is held to be the greatest curse by most of the people while the greatest sages have scorned wealth, as the greatest obstacle in the way of spiritual realization.

I am herewith giving two typical horoscopes (*In Chart No. 19*) lord of the 9th is in the 8th while lord of the 2nd is in the 12th. These two combinations have not made the person utterly poor because the 6th is not occupied by the lord of the 5th and the lord of 12th is not in the 9th while lord of the 4th is in the 4th, lord of Ascendant is in the 9th. Thus even though two com-binations for poverty are present the favourable disposition of lords of Ascendant and the 4th have acted as an antidote for poverty. The native is a middle class man.

Chart No. 19—*Born on 10-5-1903 at Gh. 27-30 after sunrise. Lat 13° N.; Long. 77° 35'. E.*

Kethu	Sun	Merc.	Venus			Jupit.	Merc. Saturn
Jupit.	Chart No. 19 RASI III-51			Moon Mars	NAVAMSA		Rahu
Saturn				Kethu			
		Ascdt. Moon	Rahu Mars		Ascdt. Venus Sun		

Balance of Rahu's Dasa at birth : years 6-7-19.

In Chart No. 20 lord of the 4th and 9th, Mars is in the 8th Mars is a Yogakarka for Leo Ascendant and his situation in the 8th has taken away the value of the horoscope. The native belongs to a respectable family but is immersed in debts.

Chart No. 20—*Born on 15-4-1883 at 1-30 p.m. Lat 30° N.; Long. 76° E.*

Mars	Sun Merc. Kethu	Saturn	Jupit.		Rahu Merc. Ascdt.	Sun Venus	
Venus	Chart No. 20 RASI III-59		Moon	Saturn	NAVAMSA		
			Ascdt.				Mars
		Rahu			Moon Jupit.	Kethu	

Balance of Rahu's Dasa at birth : years 6-7-19.

Readers must be able to differentiate between different kinds of poverty. One is born poor and

Dhana Yogas

continues to be so throughout life, while the other born in the lap of luxury suffers from the pangs of poverty by his extravagant habits and is always bothered by Creditors. I am giving the horoscope of a person who occupied a very good position as an Engineer but died grovelling in debts. He was worried by his creditors even on death bed. The combinations in the following (Chart No. 21) should be carefully noted and marked. Lord of Ascendant, Mercury is in the 8th lord of the 2nd, Moon is in the 12th with Rahu Lord of 9th Saturn is powerfully aspected by the Maraka planet Jupiter.

Marakas for different Ascendants are given in the Appendix. For further details refer to my *How to Judge a Horoscope*

Chart No. 21—*Born on 17-2-1891 at 2 p.m. (L.M.T.) Lat 13^0 N.; Long. 77^0 35' E.*

Mars	Moon Rahu	Ascdt.			Merc.	Rahu
Sun Jupit.	Chart No. 21 RASI III-61		Mars	NAVAMSA		
Merc.		Saturn	Ascdt.			Moon
Venus	Kethu			Sun Kethu	Jupit. Saturn	Venus

Balance of Mar's Dasa at birth : years 5-3-22.

अथ विद्या विचारः
Education

शुक्रश्चतुर्थंगो यस्य गानविद्या विशारदः ।
चतुर्थस्थस्सोमसुतो ज्योतिश्शास्त्र विशारदः ॥ १ ॥

Stanza 1. If Venus is in the 4th the person becomes proficient in Music. If Mercury is in the 4th the person becomes proficient in Astrology.

रविर्वा बुधराहुर्वा पंचमस्थानसंस्थिताः ।
ज्योतिर्विद्याप्रवीणस्याद्विषवैद्यवरो भवेत् ॥ २ ॥

Stanza 2. If the Sun or Mercury and Rahu be in the 5th, the native becomes learned in astrology and an expert in dealing with poisonous medicines.

द्वितीयस्थो रविबुधौ ज्योतिर्विद्याविशारदः ।
तावेव शनिना दृष्टा गणितज्ञो भवेन्नरः ॥ ३ ॥

Stanza 3. The person becomes well versed in astrology if the Sun and Mercury are in the 2nd. He becomes a mathematician if this combination is aspected by Saturn.

द्वितीयस्थौ रविकुजौ तर्कशास्त्रविशारदः ।
पचमस्थौ मन्दभानुबुधा वेदान्तपारगः ॥ ४ ॥

Stanza 4. If the Sun and Mars are in the 2nd the person becomes a logician Saturn Mercury and the Sun in the 5th make him well versed in philosophical knowledge.

बुधभानु केन्द्र कोण लाभस्थौ गणको भवेत् ।
द्वितीयस्थो यदि भृगुःकविताधर्मश्नुते ॥ ५ ॥

Stanza 5. If Mercury and the Sun are in a Kendra Trikona or the 11th house the native becomes a mathematician. If Venus is in the second house he becomes poet.

सैहिकेयः पचमस्थः गूढभावार्थवित्भवेत् ।
चतुर्थस्थ सैहिकेयः जनन्यायुष्मती भवेत् ॥ ६ ॥

Stanza 6. If Rahu is in the 5th the native will be an expert in understanding the inner meaning of things. Rahu in the 4th makes the mother long lived.

द्वितीयस्थो यदि गुरूर्वेदवेदांगपारगः ।
स्वोच्चस्वक्षेत्रयुक्तश्चेत्भवेदेवं न संशयः ॥ ७ ॥

Stanza 7. Jupiter in the 2nd makes the native an expert in Vedas and Vedangas. If such 2nd house happens to be the own of exaltation place of Jupiter, the native will undoubtedly become learned as said above and,

सभा पूज्यश्च संपूर्ण विद्यावान् भवति ध्रुवम् ।
वाक्स्थान पोवाक्पतिश्च केन्द्रकोणेषु संस्थितौ ।
सर्वविद्या प्रवीणस्यात्सभापूज्यो न संशयः॥ ८ ॥

Stanza 8. He will be honoured in public assemblies. If the 2nd lord and Jupiter are placed in a Kendra or Trikona he will be learned in different branches of knowledge and publicly honoured.

द्वितीयस्थो यदि कुजस्तर्कशास्त्रविशारदः ।
तत्रैव च भवेदिन्दुः सूत्रज्ञो यजको भवेत् ॥ 9 ॥

Stanza 9. If Mars is in the 2nd the person becomes learned in logic. If the Moon is also in the 2nd he will be a pandit or priest.

द्वितीयस्थो यदि भृगुः काव्यालंकार शास्त्रवान् ।
तत्रैवस्याद्यदि शनिर्मूढो दुष्टो भवेध्दुवम् ॥ 10 ॥

Stanza 10. Venus in the 2nd makes one learned in Kavya (poetry) and Alankara (rhetoric). He becomes vindictive evil minded and a fool if Saturn is similarly placed.

NOTES

In Sanskrit Vidya means learning and Gnana means knowledge. Knowledge is obtained not only by learning but by deep introspection. Knowledge always refers to the knowledge of the Supreme. Being Gnana is knowledge and writers on Yoga have tried to reconcile the view that liberation or Moksha is attained by means of meditation with the theory that it can be obtained by the knowledge alone. Meditation leads to Gnana or knowledge and knowledge leads to Moksha. Here when we refer to Vidya or learning we mean acquired knowledge or ideals in any branch of science or literature—erudition knowledge required by experience, scholarship, experiment and observation. Knowledge on the other hand means the clear and certain perception of truth cognition Budha is the Karaka of Vidya (learning) while Jupiter is the Karaka of Gnana or Knowledge.

In this chapter the author gives the following combinations for proficiency in the different sciences..

Music-Venus should be in the 4th house. Venus is the Karaka of Music, dancing and fine arts in general. If you examine a number of horoscopes you will find that proficiency in music can be predicted if (*a*) Venus is in the 9th or aspects the 9th house (*b*) if Venus is in the 5th or aspects the 5th house (*c*) if Venus is in the 2nd or aspects the 2nd house. Interest in music may be predicted if Venus is in the 4th from the Moon. The four combinations referred to in the above paragraphs will be found in charts underneath:—

Dhana Yogas

Chart No. 22—*Born on 12-2-1856 at 12-21 p.m. (L.M.T.) Lat 18° N.; Long. 84° E.*

	Moon Rahu	Ascdt.	Saturn		Jupit.		Ascdt.	Rahu
Sun Merc. Jupit.	Chart No. 22 RASI				NAVAMSA		
			Merc.					
Venus	Mars Kethu		Kethu			Moon Sun Saturn Venus Mars		

Balance of Venus Dasa at birth : years 6-11-3.

Chart No. 23—*Born on 7-8-1887 at 1.30 p.m. (L.M.T.) Lat 11° N.; Long. 5h. 8m. E.*

Moon			Mars		Rahu		Mars	
	Chart No. 23 RASI		Sun Merc. Rahu Saturn		Venus Sun	NAVAMSA		Moon
Kethu								
	Ascdt.	Jupit.	Venus		Jupit.	Ascdt.	Merc.	Kethu Saturn

Balance of Jupiter's Dasa at birth : years 0-7-6.

Chart No. 24—*Born on 6/7-10-1886 at 2-20 a.m., L.M.T. Lat 13° N.; Long. 77° 35' E.*

				Venus		Moon	
Kethu			Saturn	Kethu			Sun Saturn
	RASI		Rahu Ascdt.		NAVAMSA		Jupit. Rahu Ascdt.
Moon							
	Mars		Sun Merc. Jupit. Venus			Mars	Merc.

Balance of Moon's Dasa at birth : years 6-6-0.

Chart No. 25—*Born on 8-8-1912 at 7-23 p.m., L.M.T Lat 13° N.; Long. 77° 35'E.*

Rahu		Saturn Moon			Saturn	Venus	
Ascdt.			Sun	Rahu Sun			
	RASI		Mars Merc. Venus	Ascdt.	NAVAMSA		Moon Merc. Kethu
	Jupit.		Kethu		Jupit.	Mars	

Balance of Mars' Dasa at birth : years 6-0-10.

Dhana Yogas

Chart No. 26—*Born on 28-5-1903 at 1-19 a.m., L.M.T Lat 9° N.; Long. 77° 42'E.*

Ascdt. Kethu		Sun Moon Merc.	Venus	Mars		Venus Sun	Jupit. Saturn
Jupit.	Chart No. 26 RASI III-8				NAVAMSA		Ascdt. Rahu
Saturn				Kethu			Moon Merc.
			Mars Rahu				

Balance of Mars' Dasa at birth : years 6-0-10.

Astrology—(a) Mercury should be in the 4th, (b) the Sun should be in the 5th (c) the Sun and Mercury should be in the 2nd.

Vedanthaz0919(a) Saturn, the Sun and Mercury should be in the 5th, (b) Jupiter should be in the 2nd to be learned in Vedas and their Angas.

Veda is different from Vednata. I do not propose to say anything about the delicate differences existing between Veda and Vedanta in the course of these notes. I am fully aware of my incapacity to deal with such profound ideas. Vedas are the repository of knowledge while Vedanta begins where Veda ends. A glimpse of Vedanta philosophy can be had by going through the famous Brahama Sutra of Badarayana. After having obtained knowledge of karmas prescribed in the Vedas and having known that their results cannot give ever lasting bliss a time comes when a person becomes indifferent to Karmas, and therefore naturally a desire arises in him for the knowledge of Brahma WHO is above *Karma* and WHO is the source of everlasting bliss ? Vedanta gives the knowledge of the Supreme Being.

Stanza 4 gives combinations for proficiency in Vedanta while Stanza 7 deals with proficiency in Vedas and Vedangas. For understanding the Vedas properly, a thorough knowledge of the angas or auxiliaries, *viz., Siksha Vyakarna Nitruktha Chandas Tarka and Jyotisha* is essential. Astrology is an Upaveda and therefore its study is highly esteemed by the ancient writers.

Chart No. 27 – *Born on 7-5-1861 at 4-2 a.m. Lat 22° N.; Long. 88° 30'E.*

Ascdt. Moon	Sun Merc. Venus		Mars Kethu
	Chart No. 27 RASI 4-83		Jupit.
			Saturn
	Rahu		

Jupit. Ascdt.		Kethu	Merc.
	NAVAMSA		Saturn
		Moon	
	Venus Sun Rahu	Mars	

Balance of Mercury's Dasa at birth : years 9-5-22.

Poet—One becomes a poet if the 2nd house is occupied by Venus. *In Chart No. 27* Venus in the 2nd with Mercury and the Sun is exalted. This is the horoscope of one of the greatest poets of our time Venus is lord of the 3rd and the 8th. The evil due to this circumstance may find expression in different forms but the fact of the presence of Venus in the 2nd gave the native a great poetical powers.

Dhana Yogas

Diploma—Stanza 6 says that if Rahu is in the 5th the native will know the inner meaning of things. He probes into the minds of others and tries to understand their mental currents. In other words he will be a diplomat to the core. Of course diplomacy is only a dignified term for concealed hypocrisy. Personally I feel that one becomes a diplomat even if Rahu aspects the 5th house.

If Mars is in the 2nd, one becomes a logician. All people cannot become logicians in the strict sense. So it may be said that one who has Mars posited in or aspecting the 2nd be comes clever in arguments. Chart No. 28 furnishes a good illustration Mark Rahu aspecting the 5th and Mars aspecting the 2nd Stanza 10 says that if Saturn is in the 2nd the person becomes vindictive and violent, This combi-nation is also present because Saturn aspects the 2nd but this evil is greatly tempered as the 2nd is also aspected by Jupiter. All round learning can be predicted if Jupiter is in the 2nd or aspects the 2nd without any malefic aspects.

Chart No. 28 – *Born on 16-10-1918 at 2-26 p.m. I.S.T. Lat. 13° N.; Long. 77° 35'E.*

		Kethu	Jupit.			Saturn Jupit.	
Moon	Chart No. 28 RASI HJH-12			Rahu	NAVAMSA		Venus
Ascdt.		Saturn	Moon		Kethu
	Mars Rahu	Merc. Sun	Venus	Mars		Merc. Sun	Ascdt.

Balance of Rahu's Dasa at birth : years 11-8-20.

अथ भुक्ति विचारः
On Tastes or Flavours

तृतीयस्थो भवेन्मन्दः तृतीयेशयुतोपि वा ।
पश्यन्नपि तृतीयं च कट्वाम्लद्रव्यभुक्भवेत् ॥ १ ॥

Stanza 1. If Saturn is in the 3rd or he is combined with the lord of the 3rd or aspects the 3rd the person likes pungent and sour flavours.

तृतीये तु स्थितो भौमः उष्णद्रव्यिप्रयो भवेत् ।
तत्र स्थितो वाक्यतिश्चेत्सात्विक द्रव्य भुक्भवेत् ॥ २ ॥

Stanza 2. If Mars is in the 3rd the person likes hot things. If Guru is in the 3rd he likes Satvik foods.

द्वितीये यदि शुक्रस्य तांबूलादिप्रियो भवेत् ।
व्यभिचार रतश्चासीत्तत्रस्थो यदि भार्गवः ॥ ३ ॥

Stanza 3. If Venus is in the 2nd the person will be addicted to chewing betels and will have loose morals.

द्वितीयस्थो यदि शनिर्मन्दवाग्लोभवान् भवेत् ।
द्वितीयस्थो केतु गुरू वा चतु णानपणो भवेत् ॥ ४ ॥

Stanza 4. If Saturn is in the 2nd the native speaks rudely and indistinctly. If Kethu or Jupiter is there, he will be a clever speaker.

भानु भौमौ द्वितीयस्थौ वाक्कूषुकाठिन्यमुच्यते ।
द्वितीये संस्थितश्चेन्दुर्वाक्कूषु संभ्रम उच्यते ॥ ५ ॥

Stanza 5. If the Sun and Mars are in the 2nd the person will be harsh in his speech. If the Moon is there he will be very talkative.

द्वितीयस्थस्सोमसुतो युक्तियुक्तं वचो भवेत् ।
तत्रैव संस्थितो राहुः वाक्कूषुदीनत्वमुच्यते ॥ ६ ॥

Stanza 6. If Mercury is in the 2nd, he will talk cleverly and skillfully. If on the other hand Rahu is there humility will characterise his behavior.

द्वितीयस्थो यदि कविः क्षीरभक्ष्यादि भुक्भवेत् ।
तत्रस्थो राहु केतू वै समयोचित भुक्भवेत् ॥ ७ ॥

Stanza 7. If Venus is in the 2nd, the native consumes milk and varieties of dishes. If Rahu or Kethu is there, he will eat food according to circumstances.

द्वितीयस्थो यदि शनिः शूद्रान्नं कुत्सितो धनम् ।
उच्छिष्टान्नं च श्राद्धान्नं जातोह्यित्त न संशयः ॥ ८ ॥

Stanza 8. If Saturn is in the 2nd, the native gets food polluted by Sudras, remnants of food left by others and food prepared at the times of obsequies and death ceremonies.

NOTES

In this chapter the author deals with the tastes or flavours liked by different persons born with different planetary combinations. The Hindus had long ago realized that flavours or rasas developed human nature in certain channels. According to Ayurveda there are six important Rasas, viz, sweet (*madhuram*), sour (*amla*), saline (*lavana*), pungent (*khara*), bitter (*kahi*), astringent (*kashaya*). These shadrasas (six kinds of flavours) play an important part in the classification and distribution of the food after it is taken in. Sweet is nutritive and rejuvenating. It has a cooling property. If predisposes to wounds, urinary disorders and enlargements of glands in the body. Sour increases saliva and appetite for food. With Saline ducts of the body are purified. Pungent produces a burning sensation on the tongue. It clears and purifies the ducts of the body. Thus each flavor has certain properties helping in the digestion of the food. If certain planets are disposed in a certain manner the individual takes liking for certain flavours and his temperament and mental dispositions largely depend upon the likes and dislikes he shows towards the different flavours.

People who are emotional and short tempered like pungent foods. Intellectuals like sour foods and so on. There are of course exceptions. According to astrological terminology planetary relations of the different rasas are as follows:—

Planet	Rasa	Flavour
The Sun	Khara	Pungent
The Moon	lavana	Saline or Saltish
Mars	Kahi	Bitter
Mercury	Misram	Mixed
Jupiter	Madhuram	Sweet
Venus	Amla	Sour
Saturn	Kashayam	Astringent

There seems to be some difference between our author and other ancient writers on astrology in the matter of allocation of the Rasas. According to this book if Saturn is in the 3rd from Ascendant or is in conjunction with the 3rd lord or aspects the 3rd, the person likes pungent and acid flavours. The Sun rules pungent things while Venus rules sour things. Of course only one combination is given here and this as I have observed holds good in a number of horoscopes. It is incomplete and therefore readers have to attempt

Dhana Yogas

predictions by taking into account the allotment of flavours as given above.

The person eats Satvika foods if Jupiter is in the 3rd (stanza 2). Different kinds of food develop different natures in men. No one can deny that climatic influences, environmental factors and the foods we eat direct our mental currents in particular channels and develop our natures in different ways. According to astrology, the Sun the Moon and Jupiter are divine in nature and indicate Satvikaguna or a philosophic disposition Venus and Mercury represent Rajasa or imperious dispositions. Mars and Saturn denote Thamasa or mild nature.

Take a person addicted to drinks and luxurious forms of meals. He will certainly be *Rajasa*. Take a person who likes simple food and avoids all forms of luxurious and harmful dishes. His disposition will be entirely different. All these differences can be easily ascertained by a careful study of the planetary dispositions in the horoscope.

When the author says in stanzas 2nd and 3rd that the person likes Satvik foods if Jupiter is in the 3rd and that he will be loose in morals if Venus is in the 2nd, it is full of significance and should enable the intelligent reader to anticipate how the temperament of an individual stands when other planets are situated in the 2nd and 3rd houses.

The creative energy called *Prakrithi* manifested itself in three different forms producing different characters in the being in whom they are indicated. Satvika (indicated by Jupiter the Sun and the Moon) is pure and causes light and knowledge. It produces happiness and wisdom faith and love Rajasa (ruled by Venus and Mercury) denotes desires for objects and binds the soul by the chords of passionate wants Thamasa (ruled by Mars and Saturn) makes all people avaricious and causes laziness negligence and evil inclinations Satva gives moral happiness, Rajasa makes one proud and vain. Thamasa makes one bad and do evil work. The concentration of mind and its elevation depend upon the influences of the planets which obtain an ascendency at the time of birth. Planets indicate what sort of nature a man possesses. If in a man Thamasa and Rajasa predominate, provided planets denoting these respective characteristics are powerful then by proper regulation of the external influences surrounding him on Sastraic ordinances it is possible to produce desirable mental characteristics and make men Satvikas. It is on this principle that regulations in diet, in sleep, in occupations in sexual relations and in mental outlook are laid down by the Hindu sages.

Stanzas 5 and 6 reveal whether a man would be talkative, whether his speech would be harsh or pleasant and whether he could talk clearly or indistinctly and so on.

Kethu Jupiter and Mercury in the 2nd are good while the Sun, Mars and Saturn make one harsh in his speech and behavior. Rahu is the 2nd makes one humble in his addresses. In other words humility will characterise his behavior. Some say that humility is a virtue in as much as it denotes absence of egoism and self importance. Some mistake humility for cowardice. But such men are themselves mistaken. One important fact should be noted. Saturn in the 2nd is undesirable because it makes one mean, harsh, undignified, lacking self respect, quick tempered and foul tongued. Of course these results should not be predicted if the evil influences are relieved by the conjunctions and aspects of natural benefics particularly Jupiter and Venus.

Thus ends the Second Chapter entitled. "Wealth and Education" in Bhavartha Ratnakara of Sri Ramanujacharya.

Chapter 3

Brothers

भ्रातृस्थानेश्वरस्यापि भ्रातृणां कारकेण वै ।
कृजेन सह संबन्धे भ्रातृवृद्धिरुदीरिता ॥ १ ॥

Stanza 1. The existence of brothers should be divined either from the lord of the 3rd or from the karaka of brothers or from the planets combined with Mars.

विक्रमे विक्रमाधीश रविभूमिसुतास्थिताः ।
भवेद्यदि हि जातस्तु साहसी धीर उच्यते ॥ २ ॥

Stanza 2. One becomes brave and courageous if the lord of the 3rd, the Sun and Mars are in the 3rd house.

राहुकेतू तृतीयस्थौ जातस्साहसिको भवेत् ।
तत्रैव स्यात्सोमसुतो धैर्यहीनो भवेन्नरः ॥ ३ ॥

Stanza 3. The person becomes brave if the third is occupied by Rahu or Kethu. He will be timed if Mercury is in the 3rd.

बलहीने भ्रातृभावे संबन्धो गुरूभौमयोः ।
अस्तिचेत्भ्रातृ बहुलं वक्तव्यं विबुधोत्तमैः ॥ ४ ॥

Stanza 4. If the third house being weak is occupied or aspected by Jupiter and Mars the native will have brothers.

लाभस्थो यदि देवेज्यःज्येष्ठभ्रातुस्तु दुःखदः ।
लाभे च संस्थितो भौमःशनिना वीक्षितो यदि ॥ ५ ॥

Stanza 5. The person suffers sorrow from elder brother if Jupiter is in the 11th or if Mars is in the same position aspected by Saturn.

भ्रातृणां ज्येष्ठसंज्ञानां ह्यभाव:प्रोच्यते बुधै: ।
षष्ठाष्टमे भ्रात्रधीश: भ्रात्रारिष्टं तु कथ्यते ॥ ६ ॥

Stanza 6. If Mars is in the 11th aspected by Saturn the person will not have an elder brother. If the 3rd lord is in the 6th or 8th death of brothers will happen.

क्षित्रयाणां जातकेतु राज्येशे विक्रमे यदि ।
राजयोगस्य न्यूनं हि भवत्येव न संशय: ॥ ७ ॥

Stanza 7. Destruction of Raja Yoga will occur if (in the horoscopes of Kings and rulers) the 10th lord is in the 3rd.

धनादिपतिना भ्रातृनायकस्य सहस्थिति: ।
औदार्यतस्य वक्तव्यं जातकस्य बुधोत्तमै: ॥ ८ ॥

Stanza 8. The learned in astrology predict generous instincts if the 3rd lord is combined with the 2nd lord.

धन भ्रातृपतिभ्यां वा संबन्धस्सूर्यजस्यहि ।
बहुलौभ्यं हि वक्तव्यं जातकस्य सदा बुधै: ॥ ९ ॥

Stanza 9. Professors in astrology say that the person becomes a miser if Saturn is combined with 2nd and 3rd lords.

षष्ठाष्टमव्यये भ्रातृनायको यदि संस्थित: ।
तत्रैव शुभसंयुक्ते ह्यरिष्टंतु चिरात्भवेत् ॥ १० ॥

Stanza 10. If the lord of the 3rd is in the 6th, 8th or 12th, death of brothers will take place. If benefios are in these houses then death (of brothers) will take place late in life.

NOTES

The 3rd house rules brothers, sisters and courage while the 11th rules elder brothers. The stanzas are simple and are easily understandable. Mercury's presence in the 3rd makes one timid and funky while he becomes brave and courageous when the 3rd is occupied by Mars and the Sun. The presence of Rahu and Kethu in the 3rd is also suggestive of bravery and courage. If the 3rd lord is combined with the 2nd lord the native will possess generous instincts. If Saturn is connected with the 2nd and 3rd lords the person becomes a miser.

Stanzas 1, 5, 6 and 10 deal with brothers. The 3rd is the house of brothers and Mars is *Bhratrukaraka*. The presence of brothers should be ascertained from (*a*) the lord of the 3rd, (*b*) Mars and (*c*) the planet in conjunction with (or aspected by) Mars. If the 3rd house is weak but is combined with or aspected by Mars and Jupiter, the native will have brothers.

Chart No. 29—*Born on 24-8-1890 at Gh. 37-10 after sunrise Lat. 13° N.; Long. 77° 35'E.*

Ascdt.		Rahu		Kethu	Jupit.		
Jupit.	Chart No. 29 RASI III-59		Sun Saturn	Moon Merc.	NAVAMSA		Sun
				Mars			Saturn Venus
	Moon Mars Kethu		Merc. Venus		Ascdt.		Rahu

Balance of Mercury Dasa at birth : years 7-3-24.

In *Chart No. 29* the 3rd house is occupied by Rahu a malefic and aspected Saturn. This suggests that the 3rd house is weak. But note both Mars and Jupiter are aspecting the 3rd house. This is indicative of the presence of a number of brothers and sister (stanza 4) Jupiter is in the 11th from Ascendant. The 11th rules elder brother as per stanza 5, the native has an elder brother from whom no benefit is derived Rahu in the 3rd has made the person quite courageous (Stanza 3).

Chart No. 30 – *Born on 7-8-1887 at 1-21 p.m. (L.M.T.) Lat. 11° N.; Long. 5h. 8m. E.*

Moon			Mars	Rahu		Mars	
		Chart No. 30 RASI	Sun Merc. Rahu Saturn	Sun Venus	NAVAMSA		Moon
Kethu							
	Ascdt.	Jupit.	Venus	Jupit.		Ascdt. Merc.	Kethu Saturn

Balance of Mercury Dasa at birth : years 0-8-5.

Taking *Chart No. 30* Kethu is in the 3rd house and hence the 3rd bhava is vitiated Mars aspects the 3rd as also the Sun, Mercury, Rahu and Saturn. Kethu in the 3rd gives the person courage and the partial blemish of the 3rd house is overcome by Mars aspecting the 3rd. The native has brother.

In the horoscopes of rulers (stanza 2) if the 10th lord is in the 3rd the Raja Yoga becomes defunct.

Thus ends the Third Chapter entitled "Brothers" in Bhavartha Ratnakara of Sri Ramanujacharya.

Chapter 4

Conveyances and Fortune

भाग्येशो वाहनेशश्च तावुभौ लग्नगौ यदि ।
भाग्यवाहन योगोऽयमित्याहुर्गणकोत्तमाः ॥ १ ॥

Stanza 1. Astrologers say that the person possesses fortune and vehicles if the lords' of the 4th and 9th combine together in the Ascendant.

सुखस्थानं गतो वापि पश्यन्नपि गुरूर्यदि ।
बहुसौख्यमवाप्नोति जातस्तत्र न संशयः ॥ २ ॥

Stanza 2. The native will undoubtedly be extremely happy if Jupiter occupies or aspects the fourth house.

चतुर्थेश गुरू यत्र केन्द्रकोणेषु संगतौ ।
स्थितौ चेत्सुखमाप्नोति जातस्तत्र न संशयः ॥ ३ ॥

Stanza 3. There is no doubt that the person enjoys happiness if Jupiter and lord of the 4th combine in a Kendra or a Trikona.

NOTES

In the modern world every one aspires to possess a motor car—the 20th Century *vahana*. Stanza 1 says that if the lords of Ascendant and the 9th are in Ascendant, the native will not only be fortunate but will also command conveyances. We shall come to this point subsequently Stanzas 2 and 3 deal with happiness. Happiness is an elusive term. The poor man feels that the rich man is happy. A childless man feels that one with children is happy and so on. Happiness must be judged relatively. That is taking into account, the law of compensation, one may be declared to be generally happy if be commands conveniences for leading a decent and honourable life, has a loving wife, affectionate children and some name and fame. Man cannot achieve *absolute* happiness because, in the final analysis, absolute happiness is only a state of mind that can be reached by deep meditation and a completely detached attitude of life. If Jupiter aspects the 4th or is posited there, the native will be happy, (stanza 2) as also when Jupiter and lord of the 4th house and is placed in the fourth (Stanza 3). According to Stanza 3, *Jupiter* should own the 4th house Jupiter owning in Kendra is bad but if he is in a kendra or Trikona, his malefic nature obtained temporarily might either be counteracted or it might find manifestation in other ways.

Chart No. 31—*Born on 12-2-1856 at 12-21 p.m. L.M.T. Lat. $18°$ N.; Long. $84°$ E.*

	Moon Rahu	Ascdt.	Saturn	Jupit.		Ascdt.	Rahu
Sun Merc. Jupit.	Chart No. 31 RASI				NAVAMSA		
				Merc.			
Venus		Mars Kethu		Kethu		Sun Saturn Venus Mars	

Balance of Venus' Dasa at birth : years 12-3-9.

In the following horoscope (*Chart No. 31*) Jupiter aspects the 4th, as also lords of the 4th and 5th. Of course Saturn also aspects the 4th. Though the native had all the worries and woes which every human being has and will have, Jupiter aspecting the 4th gave him that inner happiness which made him impervious to all outer distractions. He felt really happy and he was justified in his claim that he was quite happy.

वाहनेशेन संयुक्तः कारको वाहनस्य तु ।
एकौ स्थिथौ वाहनेचेतू स्वल्पवाहनमुच्यते ॥ ४ ॥

Stanza 4. If Venus is in the 4th with the lord of the 4th the person will possess ordinary conveyances.

वाहनधिप शुक्रौ तु लाभे वा भाग्यभेऽपिवा ।
राज्ये वा संस्थितौवाऽपि वाहन प्रबलप्रदौ ॥ ५ ॥

Stanza 5. If Venus as lord of the 4th is in the 11th or 10th, or the 9th, the native will possess a number of conveyances.

वाहनाधिपतेर्यस्तु संबन्धो विधुना यदि ।
अश्ववाहन योगोऽयमित्युक्तो गणिकोत्तमैः ॥ ६ ॥

Stanza 6. If the 4th lord is connected with the Moon, astrologers predict possession of carriages drawn by horses.

बुधशुक्रौ चतुर्थेतु कर्किं जातस्य संस्थितौ ।
बुधदाये भृगोरन्तर्दशायां वाहनं भवेत् ॥ ७ ॥

Stanza 7. A person born in Cancer, with Mercury and Venus in the 4th, will acquire conveyances in Mercury Dasa Venus Bhukti (Budha Dasa Sukra Bhukti).

NOTES

The above four stanzas deal with the circumstances under which a man will be able to possess conveyances. The author has necessarily been brief but the combinations enable us to extend, the principles further so that they may be applied to any number of horoscopes. *Vahanakaraka* is Venus and *Vahanasthana* is the 4th. His favourable disposition indicates acquisition of vehicles.

If the 4th lord is connected with the Moon the subject will have horse drawn carriages. *In Chart No. 32* which belongs to a Maharaja, there is interchange of houses between the 1st and 4th lords. The native had a number of vahanas – motor cars, horses, horse drawn carriages, palanquins, etc., Take a number of horoscopes and study them in the light of the above principles.

Chart No. 32—*Born on 4-6-1884 at 10-18 a.m., Lat. 12° N.; Long. 76° 38' E*

Kethu		Sun Saturn Merc.		Ascdt. Kethu			Mars
	Chart No. 32 RASI HJH-12		Ascdt. Jupit. Venus		NAVAMSA		Sun Venus Saturn
			Mars	Merc.			
		Moon	Rahu			Moon Jupit.	Rahu

Balance of Mars' Dasa at birth : years 1-11-12.

अश्ववाहनकर्तास्याच्चतुर्थस्थो गुरूर्भवेत् ।
सप्तमस्थे भवेच्छुक्रः अतिकामुक उच्यते ॥ ८ ॥

Stanza 8. If Jupiter is in the 4th the native will possess horses and horse-drawn carriages. If Venus is in the 7th he will become very sensual.

चतुर्थेस्याद्यादि शनिः परदेशेन वसत्यसौ ।
छिद्रग्रहेषु वसति काठिन्यहृदयो भवेत् ॥ ९ ॥

Stanza 9. If Saturn is in the 4th, the person lives in foreign countries. He will live in old and dilapidated houses and will be hard-hearted.

NOTES

In Chart No. 32 Jupiter is powerfully aspecting the 4th. The native maintained an excellent dog-cart in the early years of this century.

In Chart No. 25 Venus is in the 7th. The native is very passionate but his passions will not be ill spent as Jupiter is in the 10th or house of Karma besides Mercury being in the 7th. Saturn has the power of doing mischief in various ways. But he will give the person in the end great fortitude, patience and forbearance. Saturn's presence in the 4th not only spoils the indications of the 4th house but also makes the native unhappy. These evil results should not be predicted if Saturn in the 4th is in conjunction with or aspected by benefits particularly Jupiter and Venus and if he also happens to be lord of Ascendant or the Moon sign.

वाहनाधिपतिर्भाग्ये भाग्येशो वाहने यदि ।
भाग्यवाहन यौगोऽयमिति तज्ञा वदन्ति हि ॥ १० ॥

Stanza 10. The learned in astrology say that a person will have *Bhagyavabana Yoga,* if lords of 4th and 9th interchange their houses.

वाहनाधिपतिर्लाभे लाभेशो वाहने यदि ।
भाग्यवाहन योगोऽयमिति तज्ञा वदन्ति हि ॥ ११ ॥

Stanza 11. Astrologers predict *Bhagyavabana Yoga* if the 4th lord is in the 11th and the 11th lord is in the 4th.

वाहनेश: पचमस्थ: पचमे वाहनाधिप: ।
भाग्यवाहन योगोऽयमिति तज्ञा वदन्ति हि ॥ १२ ॥

Stanza 12. Similar results occur if the 4th and 5th lords interchange their houses.

वाहनाधिपतिर्लग्ने लग्नेशो वाहने यदि ।
भाग्यवाहन योगोऽयमित्यूचुर्गणकोत्तमा: ॥ १३ ॥

Stanza 13. The learned in astrology predict *Bhagyavabana Yoga* if lords of Ascendant and the 4th interchange their places.

पञ्चमाधिपतिर्भाग्ये भाग्येश: पञ्चमे यदि ।
भाग्यवाहन योगोऽयमिति तज्ञा वदन्ति हि ॥ १४ ॥

Stanza 14. The learned in astrology say that *Bhagyavahana Yoga,* is caused if the 5th lord is in the 9th and the 9th lord is in the 5th.

पञ्चमाधिपतिर्लाभे पञ्चमस्थोहि लाभप: ।
भाग्यवाहन योगोऽयमिति तज्ञा वदन्ति हि ॥ १५ ॥

Stanza 15. Astrologers say that *Bhagyavahana Yoga,* is caused if the 5th lord is in the 11th and the 11th lord is in the 5th.

वाहनेशो वाहनस्थ: पचमे पञ्चमेश्वर: ।
भाग्यवाहन योगोऽयमिति तज्ञा वदन्ति हि ॥ १६ ॥

Stanza 16. Similar results will occur if lords of the 4th and 5th are in their respective houses.

भाग्याधिपो भाग्येस्यात् लग्नेशो लग्नगो यदि ।
भाग्यवाहन योगोऽयमिति तज्ञा वदन्ति हि ॥ १७ ॥

Stanza 17. Similar results should be predicted if lords of 9 and the Ascendant are in their respective houses.

पचमाधिपतिर्भाग्ये राज्ये वा भाग्यनायक: ।
भाग्यवाहन योगोऽयमिति तज्ञा वदन्ति हि ॥ १८ ॥

Stanza 18. The learned in astrology predict *Bhagyavahana Yoga*, if the 5th lord is in the 9th and the 9th lord is in the 10th.

NOTES

Bhagyavahana Yoga, simply means a combination which ensures the general fortune of the native and gives him at the same time possession of conveyances and similar comforts. The combinations given in stanzas 10 to 18 are no more than ordinary Raja Yogas in which lords of certain (benefic) houses exchange their places with other (benefic) houses. In other words, they are all *Subhaparivarthana Yogas* and they do not need any elucidation. However I shall summarise them for ready reference of the reader.

The person gets vehicles and his general fortune is assured by the following combinations :-

(1) Lord of 4 in 9 and lord of 9 in 4

(2) Lord of 4 in 11 and lord of 11 in 4

(3) Lord of 4 in 5 and lord of 5 in 4

(4) Lord of 4 in 1 and lord of 1 in 4

Conveyances and Fortune 91

(5) Lord of 5 in 9 and lord of 9 in 5
(6) Lord of 5 in 11 and lord of 11 in 5
(7) Lord of 9 in 9 and lord of 1 in 1
(8) Lord of 5 in 9 and lord of 9 in 10

By a certain interchange of positions between lords of 11 and 9, 4 and 5, 4 and 1, 5 and 9, 4 and 5, 5 and 9, 5 and 11, 9 and 10 the various *Bhagyavahana Yogas* are formed.

पञ्चमस्याधिपतिना संबंधो यदि विद्यते ।
पुत्रकारक जीवस्य पुत्रप्रावल्यमादिशेत् ॥ १९ ॥

Stanza 19. Birth of children must be predicted if Jupiter and the 5th lord are in mutual conjunction or aspect.

पुत्रकारक पुत्रेश लग्नेशाः केन्द्रकोणगाः ।
पुत्रसौख्यमवाप्नोति जातस्तत्र न संशयः॥ २० ॥

Stanza 20. The native will positively enjoy happiness from children if Jupiter, lord of the 5th and lord of Ascendant are disposed in Kendras and Thrikonas.

NOTES

The author has been very brief with regard to the 5th house having included it along with the treatment of 4th house. The native will have children and happiness on their account if lords of Ascendant and the 5th and Jupiter are in trines and quadrants.

In *Chart No. 33* lord of Ascendant is Saturn, lord of the 5th is Mercury and Putrakaraka is Jupiter. Readers will see that all these three planets are in kendras suggesting that the native will have a number of children and also happiness through them.

Chart No. 33—*Born on 8-8-1912 at 7-23 p.m., (L.M.T.) Lat. 13° N.; Long. 77° 35' E.*

Rahu	Saturn Moon			Saturn	Venus	
Ascdt.	Chart No. 33 RASI	Sun	Rahu Sun	NAVAMSA		Moon Merc. Kethu
		Mars Merc. Venus	Ascdt.			
	Jupit.	Kethu		Jupit.	Mars	

Balance of Mars' Dasa at birth : years 6-0-10.

Thus ends the Fourth Chapter entitled "Conveyances and Fortune" in Bhavartha Ratnakara of Sri Ramanujacharya.

Chapter 5

अथ शत्रुरोगादि तरङ्ग
Enemies and Diseases

अष्टमाधिपतौ लग्ने रोगदेहो भवेन्नरः ।
षष्ठेशे लग्नगे वाऽपि ज्ञाति रोगैश्च बाध्यते ॥ १ ॥

Stanza 1. If the lord of the 8th is in the 1st the person will have a sickly body. If the lord of the 6th is in the Ascendant he will be troubled by cousins and diseases.

लग्नषष्ठाधिपाभ्यान्तु सूर्यचन्द्रमसौ युतौ ।
भानुना ज्वरगण्डस्याच्चन्द्रेण जलगण्डकम् ॥ २ ॥

Stanza 2. If the Sun and the Moon are combined with the lords of the 1st and 6th, the person will have fear from fever and fear from water respectively.

कुजेन व्रणशस्त्रार्दिग्रन्थि रोगभयं भवेत् ।
बुधेन संगतौस्यातां पित्तरोगी भवेन्नरः ॥ ३ ॥

Stanza 3. If Mars is with lords of Ascendant and 6th the person suffers from wounds, weapons and plague. If Mercury is similarly disposed he will suffer from diseases due to bile.

देवेन्द्रपूज्य संयोगे रोगाभाव उदीरितः ।
शनिना यदि योगोऽयं चोराचाण्डालजं भयं ॥ १ ॥

Stanza 4. If Jupiter is similarly conjoined, the native suffers from no diseases. If Saturn is similarly combined he will have fear from thieves and low class people.

राहुणा केतुना वापि संयोगो यदि विद्यते ।
जातस्य सर्पव्याध्रादि भयं चाहुर्मनीषिण: ॥ ५ ॥

Stanza 5. If Rahu and Kethu are in conjunction with lords of Ascendant and the 6th, the native will have fear from reptiles and feline animals.

शुक्रेण सहसंयोगे कलत्रविपदं भवेत् ।
विक्रमेश युते भौमे युद्धान्निधनमुच्यते ॥ ६ ॥

Stanza 6. If Venus is with lords of Ascendant and the 6th, danger to wife is shown. If the lord of the 3rd and Mars join together he will die in war.

रोगाधिपे व्ययस्थे तु नीचादिग्रहसंयुते ।
लग्नेशे बलसंयुक्ते रोगनाशं वदेत्बुध: ॥ ७ ॥

Stanza 7. If the 8th lord is in the 12th in combination with debilitated or inimical planets and the lord of Ascendant is strong, the person's diseases will all be destroyed.

बलहीने लग्नाथाच्छत्रुस्थानाधिपे यदि ।
शुभग्रहैश्च संबन्धे शत्रुमैत्रं सभा दिशेत् ॥ ८ ॥

Stanza 8. If lord of Ascendant, happening also to be lord of the 6th, is weak but is combined with benefic planets, the native enemies will turn friends.

NOTES

In this chapter the author briefly deals with diseases and debts. The presence of the 8th lord in Ascednat is not recommended as also that of the 6th in Ascendant. In the first case the native will always suffer from disease while in the 2nd instance he will suffer not only from physical diseases but his mind will be worried due to the machinations of cousins and other relatives. The author has not made any reference to the results that would be produced if Ascendant is aspected by the 6th and (or) 8th lords if lord of Ascendant is associated with or aspected by these two lords. Probably he wants us to anticipate the results.

In the annexed horoscope (*Chart No. 34*) lord of the 8th aspects the Ascendant and lord of the 6th is associated with lord of Ascendant. The latter evil is greatly minimized because Jupiter powerfully aspects both Saturn and the Moon. As lord of 8th aspects Ascendant, the native looks somewhat sickly.

Chart No. 34—*Born on 8-8-1912 at 7-23 p.m., (L.M.T.) Lat. 13° N.; Long. 77° 35' E.*

Rahu	Saturn Moon				Saturn	Venus	
Ascdt.	Chart No. 34 RASI	Sun	Rahu Sun		NAVAMSA		Moon Merc. Kethu
		Mars Merc. Venus	Ascdt.				
	Jupit.	Kethu			Jupit.	Mars	

Balance of Mars' Dasa at birth : years 6-0-10.

Danger from fever is indicated, according to stanza 2 if the Sun is in conjunction with both the lords of Ascendant and the 6th. Similarly danger from water should be foretold if the 1st and 6th lords are with the Moon. If supposing the 6th lord happens to be either the Sun or the Moon (in case of Aquarius and Pisces Ascendant) then danger from the two sources mentioned above should not be predicted. Similarly if the 1st and 6th lords are combined with Mars there will be danger from wounds, weapons and *grandhiroga* (a disease like plague). If Mercury joins the combination of the 1st and 6th lords the native suffers from bilious trouble. If Jupiter joins, there will be no diseases. If Saturn joins this combination, there will be trouble from thieves and low class persons. If Rahu and Kethu joins the combination the person will have fear from reptiles and animals of the Felis genus such as lions, tiger, etc. If Venus joins the combination, danger to wife is indicated. The person will die in battle if the 3rd lord joins Mars (Stanza 6). So far as the combination in stanza 6 is concerned, the student must use much discretion before venturing a prediction. If the 3rd lord happens to be Mars, then the combination becomes ineffective.

The author stresses the fact that to possess good health the lord of Ascendant should be well placed while the 8th lord should be as weak as possible.

The last stanza is important. According to it even enemies become friends if lord of the Ascendant is weak but happens to be lord of 6th also and is well aspected and conjoined. This is possible in respect of Taurus and Scorpio Ascendants as Venus and Mars can become lords of the Ascendant and the 6th. The combinations are certainly thought provoking and give much food for reflective minds.

This ends the Fifth Chapter, entitled "Enemies and Debts in Bhavartha Ratnakara of Sri Ramanujacharya."

Chapter 6

अथ कलत्रकामुक तरङ्ग
Seventh House Indications

कलत्राधिपतिर्यस्तु कारकेण युतो यदि ।
क्रूरसंबन्ध रहितः कलत्रं चैकमेव हि ॥ १ ॥

Stanza 1. If the lord of the 7th is combined with Venus and has no malefic aspects or conjunctions, the person will have only one marriage.

पापग्रहस्य संबन्धः कलत्राधिपते यदि ।
कुटुंबे सप्तमे वापि स्थिताः पापग्रहा यदि ॥ २ ॥

Stanza 2. If the lord of the 7th is combined with malefic and malefic are in the 2nd and 7th.

लाभं गतो वा शुक्रश्च शुक्रो नीचं गतोऽपि वा ।
सप्तमाधिपतिष्षष्ठे व्यये वा संस्थितो यदि ॥ ३ ॥

Stanza 3. If Venus occupies the 11th or is debilitated, if the 7th lord is in the 6th or in the 12th.

कलत्रान्तरयोगोयं विद्धिः परिकीर्तितः ।
लग्ने पापग्रहयुते कलत्रान्तरभाक् भवेत् ॥ ४ ॥

Stanza 4. The native will have more than one wife. If malefic are in Ascendant, then also the native will have more than on wife.

कुटुंबदाररन्ध्रेषु चतुर्थे व्ययभेऽपि वा ।
सितः कुजश्च शुक्रश्च बलहीनो द्विदारदः ॥ ५ ॥

Stanza 5. If Saturn Mars and Venus are weak, and occupy the 2nd, 7th, 8th, 4th and 12th the person will have two wives.

कुटुंबसप्ताष्टमवाहनव्ययेष्ववस्थितोभूमिसुतस्तथैव ।
देवन्द्रपूज्यस्तु गुरू:कुटुंबे चिरात्कलत्रांतरमादिशान्ति ॥ ६ ॥

Stanza 6. Similar results have to be predicted if Mars is in the 2nd 7th 8th 4th and 12th. If Jupiter is in the 2nd, the person will have a second wife late in life.

शनि: कुटुंबे राहुश्चेत्सप्तमे यदि विद्यते ।
द्विकलत्रकयोगोयमित्याहुर्जातकोविदा:॥ ७ ॥

Stanza 7. Astrologers say that a person will have two marriages if Saturn is in the 2nd or Rahu is in the 7th.

NOTES

In Stanza 1 the author says that if the 7th lord and Venus are free from affliction the person will have only one marriage. In the next six stanzas combinations are given for two marriages. Whenever, in the course of translation, reference is made to more than one wife it should be taken to mean more than one marriage. If also implies a second marriage after the death of the first wife. The stanzas are simple enough and need no explanation at all. One important principle seems to emerge out from the above stanzas and this is the less the 7th lord and Venus are afflicted the less will be the misery and cares rising from the 7th house indications. The 2nd house is equally important because it represent *Kutumba* or family. Thus in order to have a smooth sailing in all affairs connected with family and wife, both the 2nd and 7th, their lords and Venus should be properly fortified.

Seventh House Indications

द्वितीयासप्तमेशौतु शुक्रौ वा युगसप्तमे ।
पश्यन्तशशुभसंयुक्ता यावत्संख्याग्रहैर्युताः ॥ ८ ॥

Stanza 8. If the 2nd and 7th are occupied by either the lords of the 2nd and 7th or Venus and if the 2nd and 7th are conjoined with or aspected by benefics, then the number of such benefics.

तावञ्जीव कलत्राणि क्रूरयुक्तास्तुते यदि ।
कलत्रं भागमाप्नोति चैकभार्या विशिष्यते ॥ ९ ॥

Stanza 9. Indicates the number of living wives the native will have, while only one wife will live if malefic join the above combination.

NOTES

The above two stanzas are not difficult but are only confusing. Stanzas 8 and 9 comprehend the following combinations :-

(a) If the lord of the 2nd is in the 2nd and is aspected by or combined with benefics.

(b) If the lord of the 7th is in the 7th and is aspected by or combined with benefics.

(c) If Venus is in the 2nd or 7th and aspected by or combined with benefics.

(d) If lords of 2nd and 7th are in the 2nd and 7th respectively and are aspected by or combined with benefics, then the number of living wives will correspond to the number of benefics in conjunction with or aspecting the above combinations. If however the planets, aspecting the above combinations are malefic instead of benefics then the native will have only one wife. This may mean that he may have only one surviving wife.

सप्तमस्थो यदि भृगुस्सौरिणा संयुतो यदि ।
स्वस्त्रीसक्तक इति प्रोक्तो जातो ज्योतिषकोत्तमैः ॥ १० ॥

Stanza 10. Astrologers say that if Venus is in the 7th with Saturn, the person will remain attached to his own wife.

सप्तमस्थो यदि बुधः परस्त्रीसक्त उच्यते ।
सप्तमस्थो यदि गुरूः भार्या पतिपरायणा ॥ ११ ॥

Stanza 11. Mercury in the 7th makes the person addicted to other women. Jupiter in the 7th renders the wife deeply devoted to him.

सप्तमेश कुटुंबेश कर्मेशास्तु चतुर्थगाः ।
परस्त्रीषु रतो जातः इत्यूचुर्गणिका बुधा ॥ १२ ॥

Stanza 12. Astrologers say that if the lords of the 7th, 2nd and 10th are in the 4th, the person will be addicted to other women.

सप्तमस्थः सैंहिकेयः जातेन निपुणो भवेत् ।
सप्तमस्थो यदि ध्वजः भार्या धूर्तेति कथ्यते ॥ १३ ॥

Stanza 13. The person becomes skilful if Rahu is in the 7th. Kethu in a similar situation makes the wife a shrew.

NOTES

It is very difficult to define exactly the term 'morality'. Moral values depend upon so many factors. In India, one is guilty of a moral lapse, if he sexually unites with a women other than his legal wife. In the west such a lapse is normally ignored.

The presence of Mercury in the 7th and the conjunction of the 2nd, 7th and 10th lords in the 2nd are not conducive to make the person confine his sexual pleasures to his own wife.

Thus ends the Sixth Chapter entitled "Seventh House Indications" in Bhavartha Ratnakara of Sri Ramanujacharya.

Chapter 7
अथ आयुरारोग्यतरङ्ग
Health and Longevity

संपच्छरीरपुत्राणां कारकस्य गुरोर्यदि ।
लग्नाधिपतिना योगोह्यायुः प्रबलमादिशेत् ॥ १ ॥

Stanza 1. Jupiter is the indicator (karaka) of fortune, children and body. Good longevity is indicated if he is combined with the lord of Ascendant.

आयुष्करेण शनिनाह्यष्टमाधिपतेर्यदि ।
संबन्धो विद्यते यस्य दीर्घायुर्योग उच्यते ॥ २ ॥

Stanza 2. Long life will be conferred if Saturn is in conjunction with (or aspected by) the 8th lord.

अष्टमस्थे शनौ जातो दीर्घायुर्योगमाप्नुयात् ।
अष्टमेशे लग्नकेतु अल्पायुष्यं विनिर्दिशेत् ॥ ३ ॥

Stanza 3. Long life is indicated if Saturn is in the 8th. The 8th lord in Ascendant combined with Kethu confers short life.

NOTES

The author dispenses with the question of longevity rather briefly. His observations are short, concise and full of meaning. The importance of Ascendant – indicating body, and the 8th indicating longevity is recognized.

Health and Longevity

Jupiter is said to be the karaka of 'sharira' or body. Several noted writers have opined that the Sun is the *Thanukaraka* or indicator of body. Irrespective of the fact that Jupiter is or is not the karaka of the body, his association with lord of Ascendant assures good longevity. The span of human life can be brought under four important divisions, viz., *Balarishta* or infant mortality (death before 8 years), *Alpayu* or short life (death between 8 and 32 years), *Madhyayu* or middle life (death between 33 and 75) and *Poornayu* or full life (from 75 to 120). For fuller information on the subject I would refer the readers to my *Hindu Predictive Astrology* and *How to Judge a Horoscope*.

Saturn is the *Ayushkaraka* or indicator of longevity and if he is situated in the 8th house good longevity is assured. The position of the 8th lord in Ascendant is not at all conductive for long life.

पितृकारक भानोस्तु भाग्याधिपतिना यदि ।
संबन्धो विद्यते यस्य दीर्घायुः पितुरूच्यते ॥ ४ ॥

Stanza 4. The person's father will be long lived if the Sun is combined with the lord of the 9th.

भाग्यस्थो यदि भानुस्यादल्पायुष्यं पितुस्थता ।
चतुर्थे यदि चन्द्रस्तु मातुस्यादल्पजीवितम् ॥ ५ ॥

Stanza 5. The father of the person will be short-lived if the Sun is in the 9th. The mother will be short-lived if the Moon is in the 4th house.

भाग्यस्थौ भानुभाग्येशौ आयुर्हीनो भवेत्पिता ।
लाभस्थो यदि भाग्येशौ दीर्घायुर्योगवान् पिता ॥ ६ ॥

Stanza 6. The native's father will be short-lived if the Sun and the 9th lord are in the 9th. If however the lord of the 9th is in the 11th the father will live long.

NOTES

Stanzas 4, 5, and 6 give combinations for predicting futher's longevity. These three stanzas make also clear that a Karaka in his respective Bhava destroys the indications of the said Bhava. Thus the Sun as *Pitrukaraka* (indicator of father) in the 9th house causes father's death early. However if the *Pitrukaraka* (Sun) is combined with lord of the 9th, the father lives long. It should be noted that this combination should not occur in the 9th house. However the 9th lord in the 11th promotes the longevity of the father.

These principles have to be applied very carefully as otherwise the reader is bound to go wrong. In all cases where the Sun is placed in the 9th house, early death to father cannot and should not be predicted. As a matter of fact this is only one of the four factors, viz., the 9th, 9th lord, the karaka and the planets placed in the 9th.

Chart No. 35—*Born on 16-10-1918 at 2-26 p.m., (I.S.T.) Lat. 13° N.; Long. 77° 35' E.*

		Kethu	Jupit.			Saturn Jupit.	
Moon	Chart No. 35 RASI			Rahu	NAVAMSA		Venus
Ascdt.	HJH-12		Saturn	Moon			Kethu
	Mars Rahu	Merc. Sun	Venus	Mars		Merc. Sun	Ascdt.

Balance of Rahu's Dasa at birth : years 11-8-20.

In *Chart No. 35* the Sun is no doubt in the 9th house, but early death to father cannot be predicted, because

Health and Longevity

the 9th lord is in the 10th having obtained Parivarthana – and is aspected by Jupiter. In *Chart No. 36* however the situation of the Sun in the 9th is harmful to father's long life, because the 9th lord Jupiter is in the 8th with Mercury lord of 3rd and aspected by Saturn.

चतुर्थस्थानपतिना संबन्धों यदि विद्यते ।
मातृकारक चन्द्रस्य मात्रायुष्यं विनिदशेत् ॥ ७ ॥

Stanza 7. If the Moon is combined with the lord of the 4th the mother will have long life.

Chart No. 36 – *Born on 13-3-1891 at 2-19 p.m., (L.M.T.) Lat. 13° N.; Long. 77° 35' E.*

Sun	Moon Mars	Rahu			Merc.		Rahu Venus
Merc. Jupit.	Chart No. 36 RASI	Ascdt.			NAVAMSA		Moon Sun Mars
Venus	I-89	Saturn (R)	Jupit.				
	Kethu				Kethu	Saturn	Ascdt.

Balance of Kethu's Dasa at birth : years 0-0-26.

NOTES

Compare this to stanza 4. The combination of the 4th lord and the Moon is good so far as mother's longevity is concerned but the Moon should not occupy the 4th. The Moon's situation in the 4th is decidedly harmful if he is with Saturn also In *Chart No. 37* the Moon is in the 4th in conjunction with Saturn. The 4th lord Venus is also not well disposed. Hence the native lost his mother in his second year.

Stanza 8. If Mars is in the 3rd the brothers will be short lived. If Jupiter is in the 3rd, evil is caused to brothers.

Chart No. 37—*Born on 8-8-1912 at 7-23 a.m., (L.M.T.) Lat. 13° N.; Long. 77° 35' E.*

Rahu		Saturn Moon			Saturn	Venus
Ascdt.	Chart No. 37 RASI		Sun	Rahu Sun	NAVAMSA	
			Mars Merc. Venus	Ascdt.		Moon Merc. Kethu
	Jupit.		Kethu		Jupit.	Mars

Balance of Kethu's Dasa at birth : years 0-0-26.

तृतीयस्थो यदि गुरू स्वक्षेत्रेस्यात्तृतीयकम् ।
एक एव च भ्रातास्यज्जातकस्य वदंति हि ॥ ९ ॥

Stanza 9. If the 3rd happens to be owned and occupied by Jupiter the native will have only one brother.

NOTES

In stanza 8 the author uses the term *Bhratusyadalpa Jeevitam* for Mars in the 3rd while the term used for Jupter's position in the 3rd is Bhrathrarishtam vedanthihi *Arishta* also means loss or death. But in this particular case I interpret *Aristha* as meaning evil. Thus if Mars is in the 3rd the brothers will be short lived while Jupiter in the 3rd indicates evil to brothers. In other words brother will not thrive or prosper well Stanza 9 requires that in order to have only one

Health and Longevity

brother Jupiter must be in the 3rd but also the 3rd must be a sign owned by Jupiter. This is possible only in respect of persons born in Libra and Capricorn in which case Jupiter becomes the 3rd lord.

आयुर्हीनं च पुत्रस्य गुरू: पचमगो यदि ।
अल्पायुष्यं कलत्रस्य भृगुस्सप्तमगो यदि ॥ १० ॥

Stanza 10. Jupiter in the 5th diminishes the longevity of son Venus in 7th makes the wife short-lived.

चतुर्थेशश्चन्द्रमाश्च भाग्ये राज्येऽथ लाभगे ।
पचमेहिस्थितौस्यातां मातु: दीर्घायुषं वदेत् ॥ ११ ॥

Stanza 11. Predict long life to the native's mother if the 4th lord and the Moon are in the 9th, the 10th, or the 5th.

चतुर्थेश: चतुर्थस्थ: मूलकोणं भर्वोद्हम् ।
दीर्घमायुस्समाप्नोति मातेत्यूचुबुधोत्तमा: ॥ १२ ॥

Stanza 12. The learned in astrology say that if the 4th lord is in the 4th and it happens to be Moolatrikona for the 4th lord, then the mother will be long lived.

चतुर्थेशश्च चन्द्रश्च प्रबलस्थान संस्थितौ ।
क्षीण चन्द्रो यदि भवेच्चतुर्थशनिवीक्षितं ।
अल्पायुष्यं समाप्नोति जातस्य जननी ध्रुवम् ॥ १३ ॥

Stanza 13. If the 4th lord and waning Moon, are in the 4th aspected by Saturn, in native's mother will be short lived.

NOTES

Stanza 10 only confirms the common dictum that a Karaka in his respective bhava destroys the indications of the bhava concerned Jupiter in the 5th makes the son short lived, Venus in the 7th makes the wife short lived. With due deference to the great author of this work. I have to submit that my own personal experience (which is not meager) warrants that I should respectfully disagree with the common notion that Jupiter in the 5th and Venus in the 7th are bad for those two bhavas. If Jupiter is in the 5th the native will not only have a son as the first issue but he will live long. Similarly Venus in the 7th makes the wife beautiful, fair and passionate. If Jupiter and (or) venus are afflicted by Mars the native will not derive much happiness from the sons and the wife. If Rahu or Saturn be the afflicting body, then you can predict short life to the sons or wife.

Stanzas 11, 12 and 13 are only an extension of the principle adumbrated in stanza 5, wherein it is stated that the Moon in the 4th is not conducive to the life of the mother. Under certain special circumstances the evil nature of the combination referred to in stanza 5 will be cancelled and these exceptions are dealt in stanzas 11 and 12.

Thus ends the Seventh Chapter entitled Health and Longevity in Bhavartha Ratnakara of Sri Ramanujacharya.

Chapter 8

अथ भाग्यरोगतरङ्ग
Fortunate Combinations

भाग्माधियो लाभगे वा लाभेशो भाग्यगो यदि ।
लाभ भाग्याधिपत्योश्च संबन्धे भाग्यमादिशेत् ॥ १ ॥

Stanza 1. If the lord of the 9th is in the 11th and the lord of the 11th is in the 9th or if the 9th and 11th lords are conjoined together or aspect each other, the native will be fortunate.

द्वन्द्वी भूय ग्रहश्चाटौ वेदसंख्यासु राशिषु ।
स्थितश्चेद्द्रहु भाग्यस्तु वक्तव्यो जातकस्य हि ॥ २ ॥

Stanza 2. The native will be very fortunate if eight planets occupy four houses in pairs of two each.

द्वन्द्वीभूयग्रहाषष्ठ गुणसंख्यासु राशिषु ।
स्थितश्चेद्द्राग्ययोगस्तु वक्तव्यो जातकस्य हि ॥ ३ ॥

Stanza 3. The person will be fortunate if planets occupy three signs in pairs of two each.

चतुर्णा-शुभ खेटानां पापखेटक वीक्षणम् ।
नास्ति चेद्द्राग्य बाहुल्यं धनयोगं समश्नुते ॥ ४ ॥

Stanza 4. If four benefics are aspected by malefics the person will not be very fortunate but he will have some wealth.

तृतीय षष्ठ लाभेषु स्थिताश्चेत् क्रूर खेचराः ।
जातस्य योगो भाग्यस्य वक्तव्यस्सूरिभिस्तथा ॥ ५ ॥

Stanza 5. The person becomes fortunate if malefic occupy the 3rd 6th and 11th houses.

यद्भावकारको लग्नाद्द्वये तिष्ठति चेद्यदि ।
तस्य भावस्य सर्वस्य भाग्ययोग उदीरितः ॥ ६ ॥

Stanza 6. The person will be fortunate in respect of that Bhava whose karaka is situated in the 12th from Ascendant.

NOTES

Bhagya implies fortune as different from wealth. A man may command any amount of wealth but still he cannot be called fortunate if he is devoid of children, if his relations are inimically disposed, if his wife is quarrelsome and if his reputation and name are sullied. Thus 'fortune' is an invisible

Goddess whom no wealth can court. In this chapter, the author refers to the various combinations which make a man generally 'fortunate'. According to stanza 2, a person will be very fortunate if the eight planets are situated in four houses in pairs of two each. This combination more or less corresponds to *Kedara Yoga* – one of the 7 Sankhya Yogas referred to in *Brihat Jataka*, with this difference that our author specifies the number of planets as 8, which includes Rahu also, while the author of *Brihat Jataka* has ignored Rahu in his treatment of Sankhya Yogas. The planets must occupy 4 houses in pairs of two each. Here again the reader should use his intelligence in differentiating the results. If the four signs happen to be the 7th to 10th houses then the native's fortune will be generally centered on the indications of these houses while if the four houses are 10th to 1st, the degree of fortune

Fortunate Combinations

and the source from which it flows must necessarily differ.

Stanza 4 is important because it gives a combination which while making one wealthy, renders him unfortunate. The four benefics are the waxing Moon, well associated Mercury, Jupiter and Venus. These should be free from malefic aspects.

In Chart No. 38 it will be seen that all the four benefics are subjected in some way or other to malefic aspects – the exception being that the Moon is waxing and that Saturn though a malefic is lord of the Ascendant. The original clearly says 'papakheta veekshanam' meaning 'should be aspected by malefics'. Here no reference is made to the question of association and conjunction. Therefore if we accept the combination literally, then it means that the native will not be fortunate if the four benefics are aspected by malefics and that if there is association with malefics, the evil sign in greatly minimised. This

Chart No. 38 – *Born on 8-8-1912 at about 7-23 p.m., (L.M.T.) Lat. 13° N.; Long. 77° 35' E.*

Rahu		Saturn Moon			Saturn	Venus	
Ascdt.	Chart No. 38 RASI		Sun	Rahu Sun	NAVAMSA		Moon Merc. Kethu
			Mars Merc. Venus	Ascdt.			
	Jupit.		Kethu		Jupit.	Mars	

Balance of Mars' Dasa at birth : years 6-0-10.

combination in its modified form applies to the above horoscope Jupiter is aspected by Saturn while the Moon, Mercury and Venus are not aspected. Thus the native is fortunate in regard to children, name, fame profession and money matter.

Stanza 5 says that in Upachayas (3, 6 and 11) malefic promote fortune.

Stanza 6 gives an important clue. It says that the native will be fortunate only in respect of such bhavas whose karakas are in the 12th from Ascendant. Here emphasis is laid on the *karaka of the bhava* and not on the lord of the bhava. The following are the important karakas for the different bhavas:-

Thanubhava	or	1st house	The Sun
Dhanabhava	or	2nd house	Jupiter
Bhratrubhava	or	3rd house	Mars
Matrubhava	or	4th house	The Moon
Putrabhava	or	5th house	Jupiter
Satrubhava	or	6th house	Saturn
Kalatrabhava	or	7th house	Venus
Ayurbhava	or	8th house	Saturn
Pitrubhava	or	9th house	The Sun
Karmabhava	or	10th house	Jupiter
Labhabhava	or	11th house	Jupiter
Vyayabhava	or	12th house	Saturn

Thus if the Sun is in the 12th from the Ascendant, the native will be fortunate in respect of 9th house indications, if the Moon is in the 12th, in respect of 4th house indications if Venus is in the 12th in respect of the 7th house indications and so on.

Fortunate Combinations

Chart No. 39 – *Born on 12-2-1856 at about 12-21 p.m., (L.M.T.) Lat. 18° N.; Long. 84° E.*

	Moon Rahu	Ascdt.	Saturn	Jupit.		Ascdt.	Rahu
Sun Merc. Jupit.	Chart No. 39 RASI III-85				NAVAMSA		
				Merc.			
Venus		Mars Kethu		Kethu		Moon Sun Saturn Venus Mars	

Balance of Venus' Dasa at birth : years 6-11-3.

In *Chart No. 39* the Moon Karaka for the 4th house is in the 12th from the Ascendant and hence the native was fortunate in respect of mother.

But note the Moon is with Rahu aspected by Mars. The mother died in the 12th or 13th year.

वाहनेशश्च शुक्रश्च सप्तमेश्वर भाग्यपौ ।
लाभभाग्यगतास्तेस्तु शनि संबन्धिनो यदि॥ ७ ॥

Stanza 7. If the lord of the 4th, Venus lord of the 7th and lord of the 9th are in the 11th or 9th and are aspected by or conjoined with Saturn.

तद्दशान्तदेशाकाले गजवाहन लाभकृत् ।
बृहज्जातक योगयं सूरिभिः परिकीर्तितः ॥ ८ ॥

Stanza 8. The native, will have access to elephants in the course of the period and sub-period of Saturn. This Yoga is ascribed to Brihat Jataka by the learned in Astrology.

NOTES

In the modern times very few people can think of possessing elephants and riding on them excepting a few Indian Princes and religious heads. However the Yoga may be taken to mean that one would have access to conveyances either in Saturn's Dasa or in Saturn's bhukthi provided (*a*) the lord of the 4th is in the 9th or 11th in conjunction with or aspected by Saturn, (*b*) Venus is in the 9th or 11th in conjunction with or aspected by Saturn (*c*) the lord of the 7th occupies the 9th or 11 in conjunction with or aspected by Saturn and (*d*) the lord of the 9th is in the 9th or 11th aspected by or combined with Saturn.

लग्नभाग्य चतुर्थेशाः राज्येशेन च राज्यगाः ।
अथवा लग्नदारस्थाः तेषां दायेथबांतरे ॥ ९ ॥

Stanza 9. If the lords of the Ascendant, 9th and 4th are in the 10th, 1st or 7th in conjunction with the lord of the 10th then during the periods and sub-periods of such lords.

काले सिंहासनप्राप्ति लभते बहुभाग्यभाक् ।
महत्कीर्तिं समायुक्तो भवतीत्यनु शुश्रुमः ॥ १० ॥

Stanza 10. The native will ascend the throne, becomes very fortunate and enjoy wide fame.

NOTES

This is one of the important *Maharaja Yogas* and is a rare one too. One becomes a king, enjoying fame and prosperity in the course of the Dasa or Bhukthi of the lords of Ascendant, 9th and 4th if such lords are combined with the 10th lord-all occupying the 10th house or Ascendant or the 7th.

Fortunate Combinations

पंचमे भाग्यराशौ व उच्चस्था खेचरा स्थिताः ।
जातो योगमवाप्नोति कीर्तिंचापि समश्नुते ॥ ११ ॥

Stanza 11. If an exalted planet is situated in the 5th or the 9th, the person becomes fortunate and famous.

सूर्य शुक्र बुधाः पुत्रे लाभस्थश्च भवेद्रूः ।
बुधदाये विशेषेण धनभाग्यं समश्नुते ॥ १२ ॥

Stanza 12. The native earns much wealth in the course of Mercury Dasa if the Sun, Venus and Mercury are in the 5th and Jupiter is in the 11th.

पितृकारक भानोश्च भाग्यभावेश्वरोपि वा ।
उभौ तौ व्ययगौस्यातां पितृभाग्यमुदीरितम् ॥ १३ ॥

Stanza 13. Predict fortune through father if both the Sun and the lord of the 9th are together in the 12th house.

सूर्यमेषं गतेचैव पितृभाग्यमुदीरितम् ।
तुलायां यदि वा भानुः भाग्यहीनो भवेत्पिता ॥ १४ ॥

Stanza 14. The native's father will be fortunate if the Sun is exalted. The father will be unfortunate if the Sun is debilitated.

धनुर्लग्ने तु जातस्य पितृभाग्यमुदीरितम् ।
तुलायां संस्थितोपिस्याद्रविस्तत्रैव भाग्यदः ॥ १५ ॥

Stanza 15. Predict fortune through father for a person born while Sagittarius is rising. Even if the Sun is in Libra free flow of fortune will not be obstructed.

व्ययेश भाग्यराशीश सूर्याणां संस्थितिक्रये ।
पितृस्तु भाग्ययोगश्च व्यये देवेज्य रिःफपौ ॥ १६ ॥

Stanza 16. The native's father will be fortunate if the lords of the 12th, 9th and the Sun are in the 12th, or if Jupiter and lord of the 12th are in the 12th.

NOTES

Ordinary *Dhana Yogas* are mentioned in stanzas 11 and 12. They are simple to understand and easy to apply, and hence call for no explanation Stanza 13 is more or less a repetition of the idea given in stanza 6. The native will be fortunate in respect of father, and he will be happy, if the Sun is exalted, the reverse holds good if the Sun is debilitated, This principle does not apply in case of Sagittarius Ascendant—as here the Sun will be lord of 9th and situated in the 11th causing a favourable Yoga. Some how the author seems to lay special emphasis on the fact that a Bhava shines well if the appropriate karaka is in the 12th from Ascendant. This statement of the author should be accepted with due reservation.

Let us take the Moon. He is the karaka for the 4th house. If he is in the 12th from Ascendant, it means be is in the 9th from 4th bhava. Similarly if we take Venus – karaka of 7th house, he will be in the 6th from 7th – if he is situated in the 12th from Ascendant. The 6th is an Upachaya. If we take Mars-Karaka of the 3rd he will be in the 10th-if he is placed in the 12th from Ascendant. A karaka in particularly good position from the appropriate Bhava renders the Bhava beneficial. The author must have had this idea when he formulated the general principle referred to in the above stanzas.

व्यये शुक्रस्य संस्थानं कलात्रात्भाग्यमुदेशेत् ।
व्यये चन्दस्य संस्थानं मातृभाग्यमुदीरितम्॥ १७ ॥

Fortunate Combinations

Stanza 17. The native will be fortunate in respect of wife and mother respectively if Venus and the Moon are in the 12th from Ascendant.

कुजो व्यये स्थितो यस्य भ्रातृभाग्यमुदीतिरम् ।
भाग्येशः कुवलं रिःफे पितृभाग्यमुदीरितम्॥ १८ ॥

Stanza 18. Whoever has Mars in the 12th he will be fortunate in respect of brothers. If the 9th lord is in the 12th the native will be fortunate in regard to father.

भाग्याधिपस्सप्तमस्थः भाग्ये सप्तमनायकः ।
कलत्र भाग्यमाप्नोति स्वार्जितं धनमेव च ॥ १९ ॥

Stanza 19. If the 9th lord is in the 7th and the 7th lord is in the 9th the person will be fortunate in regard to wife, and he will have self-earned wealth.

द्वितीयेश बुधष्षष्ठे ज्ञातीनां धनमश्नुते ।
केवलं तु बुधष्षष्ठे ज्ञातीनां धनमश्नुते ॥ २० ॥

Stanza 20. The native acquires money through cousins if the 6th is occupied by Mercury and the 2nd lord. If Mercury alone is in the 6th then also he will get money through cousins.

प श्रमेशोपि वागीशो उच्चस्थानस्थितो यदि ।
भाग्यवन्तस्तस्य पुत्रा इति ज्योतिषकोविदुः ॥ २१ ॥

Stanza 21. The learned in astrology opine that one's children will become fortunate if Jupiter as lord of the 5th, is exalted.

NOTES

The chapter is headed by *Bhagya Yoga* or Fortunate Combination. In other words these combinations help us to decipher as to how one could be happy and fortunate in regard to wife, brothers, cousins, parents and the like. They also reveal how gain of money is shown through different relatives. The combination mentioned in stanza 21 holds good only with reference to persons born in Leo and Scorpio Ascendants.

Thus ends of English Chapter entitled "Fortunate Combinations" in BHAVARTHA RATNAKARA of Sri Ramanujacharya.

Chapter 9

अथ राजरोगतरङ्ग
Raja Yogas

द्वितीय पधमेशौ तु द्वितीये पचमे यदि ।
भाग्यराज्येस्थितौवापि राजयोगप्रदौ श्रुतौ ॥ १ ॥

Stanza 1. Raja Yoga is caused if the 2nd and 5th lords are in the 2nd and 5th houses or in the 9th and 10th houses respectively.

धनलाभाधिपौं राज्ये दोषादि रहितौ स्थितौ ।
तयोद्र्दाये तु संप्राप्ते राजयोगप्रदौ श्रुतौ ॥ २ ॥

Stanza 2. If the 2nd and 11th lords are in the 10th free from debilitation, inimical conjunction, combustion and other evil dispositions, then Raja Yoga will be conferred on the native in the course of the Dasas of such lords.

राज्यलाभचतुर्थेषु पचमे वा स्थितो यदि ।
राजयोगप्रदो राहुस्तद्दशान्तद्र्दशासु च ॥ ३ ॥

Stanza 3. Rahu gives rise to Raja Yoga in his own Dasa and Bhukthi if he occupies the 10th, 11th, 4th or 5th house.

केतोस्तृतीय संस्थानं योगदं भवति ध्रुवम् ।
भाग्यापत्यस्थ केतुस्तु न शुभो दोषमावहेत् ॥ ४ ॥

Stanza 4. Kethu in the 3rd will certainly give rise to Yoga. If he is in the 9th or the 5th, he becomes inauspicious and causes evil.

तृतीये चन्द्रशुक्रौ तु स्थितौचेद्योगदो भृगुः ।
शुक्रदायेतु संप्राप्ते शुक्राद्योगं समश्नुते ॥ ५ ॥

Stanza 5. Venus becomes a Yogakaraka if the Moon and Venus are in the 3rd. During Venus Dasa fame will be conferred.

राज्याधिपस्तृतीये च लाभे वा यदि संस्थितः ।
सर्वत्र योगो न भवेत्कुत्रचिच्च भविष्यति ॥ ६ ॥

Stanza 6. If the 10th lord is in the 3rd or the 11th, no permanent Yoga is given rise to. There will be slight Yoga at some time.

राज्याधिपोपि च गुरूस्तृतीये यदि संस्थितः ।
भ्रातृशत्रु यथा योगः कथययोगप्रदो गुरूः ॥ ७ ॥

Stanza 7. If Jupiter happening to be lord of the 10th is in the 3rd, he will give rise to the same Yoga that he would do, were he lord of the 3rd.

NOTES

Raja Yoga means a combination indicating political power, fame and prosperity. It is very difficult to define the world *Raja Yoga.* Yoga in Sanskrit means a combination or configuration of planets and Raja Yoga implies special combination denoting political power and fame. Raja Yogas are many and have several gradations. A village magistrate, a tribal chief, a monied man, an influential landlord, a petty king, an independent prince and a great emperor have all Raja Yogas as also the president of republic and the manager of large manufactory. Thus Raja Yoga means exercise of some power political, religious, administrative, magisterial or executive. To get real political power the Sun, the Moon and Mars must be powerful. Political power is different from power of learning, of money, personal influence and indescribabale tact. We see often in our experience men without money, without Government service, without landed properties wielding a power over their fellow-subjects, quite inexplicable. His power is not based on any temporal advantages. Readers must look to the sources of strength and weakness of the planets causing the *Raja Yoga* and then prescribe the rank. Raja Yoga may be taken to mean power and fame.

The combinations given in the chapter are indeed full of significance. As the stanzas are simple, they do not require any further elucidation.

Chart No. 40 – *Born on 12-2-1856 at 12-21 p.m.,(L.M.T.) Lat. 18° N.; Long. 84° E.*

	Moon Rahu	Ascdt.	Saturn	Jupit.		Ascdt.	Rahu
Sun Merc. Jupit.	Chart No. 40 RASI				NAVAMSA		
Venus		Mars Kethu		Kethu		Moon Sun Saturn Venus Mars	

Balance of Venus' Dasa at birth : years 6-11-3.

In Chart No. 40 note there is a conjunction of the 2nd and 11th lords viz., Mercury and Jupiter in the 10th, free from affliction. This has given rise to a powerful

Raja Yoga (vide Stanza 2). My book "How To Judge A Horoscope" deals with Raja Yoga rather exhaustively and the reader may refer to it for fuller explanations. The principles contained in the above stanzas may be summed up as follows for the information of the reader.

(1) Lords of the 2nd and the 5th should be in the 2nd and the 5th or in the 9th and the 10th to cause Raja Yoga.

(2) The 2nd and 11th lords should be in the 10th free from affliction.

(3) Rahu should be in the 10th, 11th, 4th or 5th to confer Raja Yoga in his Dasa.

(4) Kethu's presence in the 3rd is good but inauspicious in the 9th and 5th.

(5) Venus becomes capable of conferring power if he is in the 3rd with Moon.

(6) The native does not always wield power if the 10th lord is in the 3rd or the 11th but will do so only temporarily.

Illustrative of some of the combinations given above are the following charts:

In Chart No. 41 it will be seen that lord of the 2nd Mercury is in the 2nd and that of the 5th is in the 5th. This has no doubt given rise to Raja Yoga especially because Mercury the 2nd lord is exalted. But Jupiter's association with Kethu going under the technical name of *Guruchandala Yoga* has somewhat marred the Raja Yoga.

Chart No. 41—*Born on 10-9-1889 at about sunrise, Lat. 13° N.; Long. 77° 35' E.*

Moon			Rahu || Rahu	Mars	Saturn	Jupit.
	Chart No. 41 RASI HJH-53		Venus			NAVAMSA		Merc. Moon
			Mars Sun Saturn Ascdt.					
Kethu Jupit.			Merc. || Venus	Sun Ascdt.		Kethu

Balance of Jupiter's Dasa at birth : years 1-1-13.

Chart No. 41 given above illustrates the Raja Yoga mentioned in stanza 1. In Chart No. 42 given herewith Jupiter is lord of the 2nd and the 11th and he is in the 10th. This is a very auspicious combination in as much as finance, and means of livelihood are brought together so that all these three functions are

Chart No. 42—*Born on 8-8-1912 at about 7-23 p.m. (L.M.T.) Lat. 13° N.; Long. 77° 35' E.*

Rahu		Saturn Moon				Saturn	Venus	
Ascdt.	Chart No. 42 RASI III-54		Sun	Sun Rahu		NAVAMSA		Moon Merc. Kethu
			Mars Merc. Venus	Ascdt.				
	Jupit.		Kethu			Jupit.	Mars	

Balance of Mars' Dasa at birth : years 6-0-10.

promoted Jupiter Dasa in the case of the native of *Chart No. 42* has produced very beneficial results in respect of money, fame, profession and gains.

In *Chart No. 42* it will be seen that lord of the 2nd and that of the 5th is in the 5th. This has no doubt given rise to Raja Yoga especially because Mercury the 2nd lord is exalted. But Jupiter's association with Kethu going under the technical name of *GuruchandalaYoga* has somewhat marred the Raja Yoga.

Chart No. 42 given above illustrates the Raja-Yoga mentioned in stanza 2. In *Chart No. 43* given herewith Jupiter is lord of the 2nd and 11th and he is in the 10th. This is a very auspicious combination in as much as finance gains

Chart No. 43—*Born on 7-5-1861 at about 4-2 a.m. (L.M.T.) Lat. 22° 40' N.; Long. 88° 30' E.*

Ascdt. Moon	Sun Merc. Venus	Mars Kethu	Jupit. Ascdt.		Kethu	Merc.
	Chart No. 43 RASI 4.83	Jupit.		NAVAMSA		Saturn
		Saturn	Moon			
Rahu				Venus Sun Rahu	Mars	

Balance of Mercury's Dasa at birth : years 9-5-22.

This horoscope (*Chart No. 43*) illustrates the principle adumbrated in stanza 3 that Rahu in the 10th house confers Raja-Yoga in his Dasa Rahu by himself is not capable of giving rise to any results. He gives

Raja Yogas

the effects of the lord of Rasis which he occupies. Consequently, in this particular chart Rahu must cause the result of Jupiter who as lord of Ascendant and the 10th lord is exalted in the 5th. This is a unique combination which has made the subject a great figure in the field of poetry and literature.

According to Stanza 6, if the 10th lord is in the 3rd the native does not always enjoy Raja Yoga but will do so only temporarily. In this horoscope (*Chart No. 44*) the 10th lord Venus is in the 3rd in his own house with Mercury lord of finance. The native was once very well off and commanded much influence but now he is humble. Mark the Dwirdwadasa positions of planets.

Chart No. 44—*Born on 29-9-1888 at about 4-35 a.m. (L.M.T.) Lat. 26° 30' N.; Long. 74° 45' E.*

			Moon			Sun	Moon
	Chart No. 44 RASI		Saturn Rahu	Saturn Kethu	NAVAMSA		
Kethu			Ascdt.	Mars			Rahu
	Mars Jupit.	Merc. Venus	Sun	Merc. Ascdt. Venus		Jupit.	

Balance of Jupiter's Dasa at birth : years 5-5-23.

Stanza 7 is rather vigue. It says that if Jupiter as 10th lord (which is possible in case of Gemini and Pisces Ascendants) is in the 3rd, he would give rise to the same Yoga as he would do, if he were lord of the 3rd. What results Jupiter would give as lord of the 3rd

the author has not elucidated. We have to take the information from other books.

भाग्याधिपश्चाष्टमस्थस्तद्दाये नैवयोगदः ।
भाग्याधिपोपि च गुरोर्ह्यष्टयस्थोपि भाग्यदः ॥ ८ ॥

Stanza 8. If the 9th lord is in the 8th, his Dasa will not confer any fame. If Jupiter as lord of the 9th is in the 8th the person becomes highly fortunate.

NOTES

This is an important stanza not only as enunciating a general principle but as pointing out an exception. Thus the 9th lord in the 8th is not good. But Jupiter is an exception. In our humble experience we have found that if Jupiter, even without being lord of the 9th, is in the 8th the native enjoys much wealth. But such Jupiter should be lord of Ascendant. The following horoscope (*Chart No.45*) illustrates this principles.

Chart No. 45—*Born on 31-1-1986 at about 4-40 a.m. (L.M.T.) Lat. 22° 20' N.; Long. 73° E.*

			Moon			Sun Saturn
Merc. Rahu	Chart No. 45 RASI	Moon Jupit.	Rahu	NAVAMSA		Venus
Sun	III-112	Kethu				Kethu Mars
Ascdt. Mars Venus		Saturn		Merc.	Jupit.	Ascdt.

Balance of Mercury's Dasa at birth : years 2-3-1.

The Ascendant is Sagittarius and the lord Jupiter is exalted in the 8th. There are of course several other

Raja Yogas

good combinations but this one has made the native amass much fortune.

रंध्रभाग्याधिपत्योश्च संबन्धो यदि विद्यते ।
अष्माधिपतेद्र्दांये संप्राप्ते योगमादिशेत् ॥ ९ ॥

Stanza 9. If the 8th and 9th lords are in conjunction or aspect each other, fame and power will be conferred in the Dasa of the 8 lord.

NOTES

This combination is to be found in *Chart No. 45* given above. The Sun and the Moon lords of 9th and 8th respectively aspect each other so that the Moon's Dasa will confer fame and prospenty on the native.

भाग्येशदाये संप्राप्ते नैवयोगप्रदोह्यसौ ।
अष्टमाधिपतेरंतद्र्दशायां योगदो भवेत् ॥ १० ॥

Stanza 10. If the 9th and 8th lords combine with or aspect each other fame and power will be conferred not in the Dasa of the 9th lord in the sub-period of the 8th lord.

NOTES

In stanza 9, it is stated that the 8th lord gets the power to produce Yoga which means the 9th lord delegates his power to the 8th lord with the result he himself becomes powerless.

राज्यलाभाधिपत्योश्च संबन्धो यदि विद्यते ।
लाभाधिप दशाकाले राजयोगो भविष्यति ॥ ११ ॥

Stanza 11. If the 10th and 11th lords combine with or aspect each other, Raja Yoga will be caused in the Dasa of the 11th lord.

राज्यलाभाधिपत्योश्च संबन्धो यदि विद्यते ।
राज्येशदाये संप्राप्ते समयोग उदीरितः ॥ १२ ॥

Stanza 12. If the 10th and 11th lords combine with or aspect each other, good and bad results will be equal during the Dasa of the 10th lord.

लाभेशान्तर्दशाकाले योगहीनो भवेत् ध्रुवम् ।
दशमस्थ भृगोः पाके न योगं लभते नरः ।
सप्तमस्थः शनेः पाके राजयोगं समश्नुते ॥ १३ ॥

Stanza 13. The person will be deprived of fame and prosperity in the sub-period of the 11th lord. When Venus is in the 10th no Yoga will be produced in his Dasa Raja Yoga will be conferred in Saturn Dasa if Saturn is in the 7th house.

NOTES

In *Chart No. 46* note lord of the 10th aspects the lord of the 11th while for Chandra Ascendant lords of the 10th and 11th aspect each other mutually. The native

Chart No. 46—*Born on 8-8-1912 at about 7-23 p.m. (L.M.T.) Lat. 13° N.; Long. 77° 35' E.*

Rahu		Saturn Moon			Saturn	Venus	
Ascdt.	Chart No. 46 RASI		Sun	Sun Rahu	NAVAMSA		Moon Merc. Kethu
			Mars Merc. Venus	Ascdt.			
	Jupit.		Kethu		Jupit.	Mars	

Balance of Mars' Dasa at birth : years 6-0-10.

has been enjoying Raja Yoga in the Dasa of Jupiter lord of the 11th (stanza 11). The principle given out in stanza 13 that the sub period of the lord of the 11th would deprive the native of Raja Yoga is applicable in to the above example. In the sub period of Jupiter (in the Dasa of Jupiter) the native lost fame and money and his reputation was at stake for no fault of his There was a clear break in the Raja Yoga.

सप्तमस्थस्सैहिकेयो योगदो भवति ध्रुवम् ।
तृतीय भाग्यगो मन्दो योगप्रद इति स्मृतः ॥ १४ ॥

Stanza 14. Rahu in the 7th will certainly confer fame and prosperity. Saturn in the 3rd and 9th will also confer Yoga.

तृतीयाष्टम भाग्यस्थो गुरूर्योगप्रदो भवेत् ।
द्वादशस्थो यदि गुरूर्देवलोकं समश्नुते ॥ १५ ॥

Stanza 15. Jupiter in the 3rd, 8th and 9th will confer fame and prosperity. The person goes to heaven after death if Jupiter is in the 12th.

भाग्यराज्याधिपौ राज्ये भाग्ये व यदि संस्थितौ ।
राजयोगमवाप्नोति महतों कीर्तिमश्नुते ॥ १६ ॥

Stanza 16. If the 9th and 10th lords, are in the 10th and 9th respectively the native will enjoy Raja Yoga and much fame.

NOTES

The Yogas mentioned in stanzas 14 and 15 are simple enough. Contrary to the commonly accepted notion that Saturn destroys the bhava he occupies, the author holds that Saturn in the 9th confers Yoga. But readers will have to note that such a situation of Saturn would adversely affect the father. The 12th

represents *moksha* or emancipation. As Jupiter is a Deva planet, his situation in the 12th takes the person to heaven after his death.

The combination given in stanza 16 goes under the name of *Dharmakarmadhipa Yoga* or exchange of houses between 9th and 10th lords and it is an auspicious combination. Though it may not give much fame it will certainly confer prosperity and wealth.

In this horoscope (*Chart No. 47*) lord of the 9th Mercury is in the 10th while the 10th lord Venus is in the 9th. Though Venus is debilitated, he is free from debilitated effect. The native is very well off in life and enjoys much prosperity.

Chart No. 47—*Born on 16-10-198 at about 2-26 p.m. (I.S.T.) Lat. 13° N.; Long. 77° 35' E.*

	Kethu	Jupit.			Saturn Jupit.	
Moon	RASI HJH-12		Rahu	NAVAMSA		Venus
Ascdt.		Saturn	Moon			Kethu
	Mars Rahu	Sun Merc.	Venus	Mars	Merc. Sun	Ascdt.

Balance of Rahu's Dasa at birth : years 11-8-20.

राज्यस्था यदि भाग्येशः राज्येशो भाग्यगो यदि ।
राजयोगमवाप्नोति महतीं कीर्तिभश्नुते ॥ १७ ॥

Stanza 17. If the 9th lord is in the 10th and the 10th lord is in the 9th the native enjoys much fame and power.

NOTES

This is merely a repetition of stanza 16 in a different form and is quite unnecessary.

भाग्याधिपो भाग्यगतो राज्येशो राज्यगो यदि ।
राजयोगमवाप्नोति महतीं कीर्तिमश्नुते ॥ १८ ॥

Stanza 18. The person enjoys much fame and power if the 9th lord is in the 9th and the 10th lord is in the 10th.

राज्येश पचमेशौतु राज्ये वा पचमेथवा ।
स्थितौ चेद्योगमाप्नोति महतीं कीर्तिमश्नुते ॥ १९ ॥

Stanza 19. Power and fame are conferred if the 10th and 5th lords are in the 10th and 5th.

भाग्यराज्याधिपौ यत्र सप्तमस्थौ च लग्नगौ ।
राजयोगमवाप्नोति महतीं कीर्तिमश्नुते ॥ २० ॥

Stanza 20. Power and fame are conferred if the 9th and 10th lords are in the 7th and 1st houses respectively.

रिपुसप्तम राज्येशाः केन्द्रस्था यदि कोणगाः ।
राजयोगं च लभते महतीं कीर्तिमाप्नुयात् ॥ २१ ॥

Stanza 21. If the 5th, 7th and 10th lords are situated in quadrants or trines, the person enjoys power and much fame.

मैषे रवि कर्कटस्थौ जीवचन्द्रौ तुला शनि ।
मकरस्थौ भवेत्भौमो राजयोग उदीरितः ॥ २२ ॥

Stanza 22. Raja Yoga is caused if the Sun is in Aries, Jupiter and the Moon are in Cancer, Saturn is in Libra and Mars is in Capricorn.

NOTES

Stanzas 18 to 20 inclusive suggest the combinations which confer Raja Yoga. Such combination are to be found in almost all horoscopes of any pretence to power. The 10th, 9th, 5th, 7th and the 1st houses are taken into account and certain dispositions of these lords are said to confer Raja Yoga.

It is not clear as to why the 6th lord is given importance along with the 7th and 10th lords in stanza 21. Probably the 6th lord will lose the evil of 6th lordship if he is in a Kendra or trikona but still the evil will be there and it will manifest in some shape in the period or sub period of the 6th lord.

	Sun		
	Chart No. 48 III-58		Moon Jupit.
Mars			
		Saturn	

The combination given in the last stanza is to be found in very rare and ex-ceptional cases as for instance in the horoscope of Sri Rama.

The Moon and Jupiter are in Cancer. The Sun is in Aries, Saturn is in Libra and Mars is in Catricorn thus causing a very powerful Raja Yoga. The same combination will be found in the horoscopes of several well known Emperors of Puranic fame.

Raja Yogas

अथ गंगादिपुण्यस्नान योगः
COMBINATIONS FOR DIPS IN SACRED WATERS

कर्मकारक देवेन्द्र पूजयस्य यदि विद्यते ।
संबन्ध कर्मनाथेन सत्कर्मनिरतो भवेत् ॥ १ ॥

Stanza 1. If Jupiter is combined with or aspected by the lord of the 10th the native will be engaged in good deeds.

कळत्रपुत्रभाग्येशः गुरूकर्माधपतौ तथा ।
जलराशि स्थिता सर्वेह्यान्योन्यसंगता यदि ॥ २ ॥

Stanza 2. If the lords of the 7th 5th 9th Jupiter and 10th are all combined in an aquatic sign (Jalarasi).

गुरूदाये च संप्राप्ते गंगातुल्यनदीषु च ।
स्नानसिद्धिर्भवेत्सेव गंगास्नानं न सिद्ध्यति ॥ ३ ॥

Stanza 3. The native will have dips in rivers as sacred as Ganges but in Ganges in the course of Jupiter Dasa.

पुत्रदारेशदायेतु यात्राकार्यं न सिद्ध्यति ।
पुण्यश्लोकस्य विष्णोश्च कथासु निरतो भवेत् ॥ ४ ॥

Stanza 4. No pilgrimage will be undertaken in the Dasas of the 5th and 7th lords. The native will devote himself to listening to the stories of Vishnu.

युग्मजातस्य भाग्यस्थौ गुरूमन्दौ तयोर्दशा ।
काले भवति गंगायाः स्नानं भवति निश्चयः ॥ ५ ॥

Stanza 5. A person born in Gemini Ascendant will certainly have dips in Ganges in the Dasas of Jupiter and Saturn if they are in the 9th house.

मेषलग्ने तु जातस्य शुक्रेज्यार्यम्णो यदि ।
राज्यस्थास्तद्दशाकाले गंगास्नानं भविष्यति ॥ ६ ॥

Stanza 6. A person born in Aries Ascendant will bathe in Ganges in the Dasas of Venus, Jupiter and the Sun if the are in the 10th house.

कर्माधिपो गुरूयुतः कर्मप्राबल्यमादिशेत् ।
षष्ठव्ययस्थः कर्मेशः कर्महीनो भवेन्नर : ॥ ७ ॥

Stanza 7. If the 10th lord is combined with Jupiter the native will be highly religious or orthodox. If the 10th lord is in the 6th or 12th he will not be religious.

NOTES

That a separate chapter should be devoted to giving combinations for bathing in sacred rivers shows the importance which the Hindus have attached from time immemorial to the question of pilgrimage. Careful study reveals that pilgrimage to which a religions touch was given was undertaken as part of education. Pilgrimage is the final phase of education, and it has its own moral, intellectual and social values. The waters of Ganges and several other sacred rivers are full of medicinal virtue and a dip in these rivers is held so sacred that it washes not only the physical dirt but the mental impurity also. Even now, the majority of the Hindus or for that matter people of all religions years to undertake pilgrimages so that their existence on the earth might be justified.

The first stanza says that if the 10th lord and Jupiter are conjoined together or aspect each other the native will be engaged in *Satkarmas* or good deeds. Jupiter is the Guru or preceptor of the Gods and as the 10th is the house of action, Jupiter's connection with it or its lord is bound to have very favourable influences. Human nature takes different moulds. There are people who are always for destruction, wicked acts, selfishness and engaged in dirty and scandalous things Jupiter in the 10th generally counteracts this evil influence and makes the native fear God and hate injuring others, detest evil company and engage himself in charitable acts and deeds.

Chart No. 49—*Born on 8-8-1912 at about 7-23 p.m. (L.M.T.) Lat. 13° N.; Long. 77° 35' E.*

Rahu		Saturn Moon			Saturn	Venus	
Ascdt.	Chart No. 49 RASI III-54		Sun	Rahu Sun	NAVAMSA		
			Mars Merc. Venus	Ascdt.			Moon Merc. Kethu
	Jupit.		Kethu		Jupit.	Mars	

Balance of Mars' Dasa at birth : years 5-6-15.

In *Chart No. 49* Jupiter—the *Karmakaraka*—is in the 10th. In Jupiter's Dasa in his own bhukthi the native had dips is not only the Ganges but also in other sacred rivers and visited a number of holy places.

Thus ends the Ninth Chapter entitled "Rajayogas" in Bhavartha Ratnakara of Sri Ramanujacharya.

Chapter 10

अथ मारकतरङ्ग
Combinations for Death

व्ययेशस्य दशाकाले धनेशो मारको भवत् ।
द्वितीयेश दशाकाले व्ययेशो मारको भवेत् ॥ १ ॥

Stanza 1. The 2nd lord becomes a Maraka in the Das of the 12th lord. The 12th lord becomes a Maraka in the Dasa of the 2nd lord.

व्ययनाथ दशाकाले द्वितीयेशेन संगताः ।
द्वितीयेशेन दृष्टाश्च मारकप्रबलश्रुताः॥ २ ॥

Stanza 2. If the 12th lord is aspected by or is in conjunction with the 2nd lord he becomes a powerful maraka in his Dasa.

द्वितीयेश दशाकाले व्ययस्थनस्थिता खगाः ।
व्ययाधिपतिना दृष्टाः प्रबला मारकश्रुताः ॥ ३ ॥

Stanza 3. The planets in the 12th house which are aspected by the 12th lord become powerful marakas during the Dasa of the 2nd lord.

NOTES

Maraka or death is an important event in the life of an individual. I have dealt with this question fairly exhaustively in my books *Hindu Predictive Astrology* and *How to Judge a Horoscope*. The ancient seers have given a number of methods—mathematical as well

Combinations for Death

as predictive for finding the duration of life of an individual. As far as my humble experience goes, the mathematical methods have their own pitfalls and do not seem to yield correct results in the majority of cases. The predictive processes on the other hand, if handled properly by an expert who has developed intuition will be very helpful in finding the time of death.

Whatever be the combinations given for finding the maraka planets one should first ascertain, whether a horoscope in question indicates *Balarishta* (early death), *Alpayu* (short life) *Madhyayu* (middle life) or *Purnaya* (full life). Generally speaking if the majority of the planets are disposed in Kendras or quadrants, one will have long life. If in *Panaparas* (cadent houses) middle life; and if in *Apoklimas* (succeedant houses) short life. This is only a general principle and it should be applied with great care. There are well known principles which will enable any reader of average intelligence to judge the kind of Ayurdaya and they can be studied from any standard book.

The author of this work, Sri Ramanuja has given beautiful combinations. According to him—

(a) The 2nd lord becomes a maraka in the Dasa of the 12th lord and *vice versa*. This means that death will be caused in the sub period of the 2nd lord if the 12th lord happens to be a maraka. Similarly, death will be caused in the sub period of the 12th lord if the 2nd lord happens to be a maraka. The 12th or 2nd lord may become marakas by virtue of association with or being aspected by the 7th or 2nd lords. I have been a little round about in my explanation because stanza I says that the 2nd lord becomes Maraka in the Dasa of the 12th lord. How can the 2nd lord cause maraka unless as sub lord in the Dasa of the 12th lord. This clearly means that the 12th lord must also become a maraca.

(b) The 12th lord becomes a powerful maraka in the Dasa if he is associated with or aspected by the 2nd lord.

(c) Maraka can tale place in the sub periods of the planets occupying the 12th and who are aspected by the 12th lord within the Dasa of the 2nd lord.

व्ययनाथ दशाकाले तत्रस्थाः पापिनाः खगाः ।
तेषां अन्तर्दशाकाले मारकास्तु भवन्ति ते ॥ ४ ॥

Stanza 4. Death may take place in the sub-periods of malefic occupying the 12th within the Dasa of the 12th lord.

द्वितीयराशिस्थितपापखेटा दशाविपाके व्ययनाथ संगताः ।
तन्भुक्तिकाले च त एव पापिनो ग्रहस्तथा मारकनायकस्युः
॥ ५ ॥

Stanza 5. Malefic planets who are in the 2nd house in conjunction with the 12th lord will cause death in their own Dasa and bhukthi.

व्ययराशिस्थ पापिनां दशाकाले तु मारकः ।
द्वितीयाधिप संबन्धी सचराः पापिनो ग्रहाः ॥ ६ ॥

Stanza 6. Death will be caused in the Dasa periods of malefic placed in the 12th house. Planets in association with the 2nd lord will also become evil.

NOTES

Stanzas 3 to 6 inclusive are an extension of the principles given in the 1st three stanzas, with slight

Combinations for Death

variations, suggesting the circumstances under which the 12th and 2nd lords become marakas. The author seems to be inclined to the view that the 12th lord gets empowered to kill, by his association with the 2nd lord or (evil) planets in the 2nd house. Obviously it means that good planets in the 2nd house even if they are aspected by or associated with the 12th lord cannot become maracas (unless of course they get death inflicting power otherwise).

अष्टमेश दशाकाले तत्भुक्तौ सोपि मारकः ।
षष्ठेशदाये निधनं रन्ध्रेशान्तर्हुतो भवेत् ॥ ७ ॥

Stanza 7. Death will be caused by the 8th lord in his own Dasa and Bhukthi. Death will also be caused in the sub-period of the 8th lord within the Dasa of the 6th lord.

अष्टमेश दशाकाले षष्ठराशिस्थ पापिनाम् ।
हृतौ जातस्य निधनं वदन्ति विबुधोत्तमाः ॥ ८ ॥

Stanza 8. Astrologers opine that death will be caused by malefics in the 6th, in their sub-periods.

षष्ठनाथ दशाकाले अष्टमस्थ खगस्य च ।
हृतौं जातस्य निधनं वदन्ति विबुधोत्तमाः ॥ ९ ॥

Stanza 9. Astrologers predict death to the native in the Dasa of the 6th lord and sub-period of the 8th lord.

अष्टमेश दशाकाले अष्टयेशेन वीक्षिताः ।
षष्ठेश संगता ये च तान्वदन्ति हि मारकान् ॥ १० ॥

Stanza 10. Planets who are aspected by the 8th lord and planets who are associated with the 6th lord become marakas in the Dasa of the 8th lord.

अष्टमास्थितपापस्य दशाकाले वदन्ति हि ।
षष्ठस्थानपतेरन्तर्दशाकालो हि मारकः ॥ ११ ॥

Stanza 11. Death will be caused in the Dasa of a malefic occupying the 8th and the sub-period of the 6th lord.

षष्ठस्थितस्य पापस्य दशाकाले वदन्ति हि ।
अष्टमाधिपतेरन्तर्दशाकालो हि मारकः ॥ १२ ॥

Stanza 12. Death will happen in the Dasa of a malefic occupying the 6th house and the sub-period of the 8th lord.

षष्ठस्थितस्य पापस्य दशाकालो वदन्ति हि ।
अष्टमस्थित रन्ध्रेश भुक्तिकालो हि मारकः ॥ १३ ॥

Stanza 13. Death will occur in the Dasa of a malefic occupying the 6th and in the sub-period of the 8th lord placed in the 8th house.

अष्टमस्थित पापस्य दशाकाले वदन्ति हि ।
षष्ठस्थितस्य पापस्य भुक्तिकालो हि मारकः ॥ १४ ॥

Stanza 14. Death will happen in the Dasa of a malefic occupying the 8th and in the Bhukthi of a malefic posited in the 6th.

NOTES

Stanzas 7 to 14 inclusive describe combinations which cause death by certain dispositions of the 6th and 8th lords. The 6th is the house of disease and the 8th is the house of life or Ayus. In all the above principles, no reference is made to the 7th lord. For the information of the reader I may just enunciate the general principles governing maraka. The author of this work has given some importance to the lord of

Combinations for Death

the 8th and 6th. But in the general principles, the 6th and 8th lords become of importance because death is to be predicted in their Dasas provided, the Dasas of other planets declared as Marakas are not likely to operate Prof. B. Suryanarain Rao's English Translation of Jathaka Chandrica make these principles very clear.

(1) Lord of the 2nd or 7th is a maraka.
(2) Malefic occupants of these two houses.
(3) Malefic planets in association with these lords.
(4) Denefics in association with the 2nd and 7th lords.
(5) Lords of 7th and 8th.
(6) Lord of 3 or 8 associated with the 2nd or 7th lord.
(7) Saturn in association with a marka.
(8) Lord of the 6th or 8th whether or not he is associated with a maraca.
(9) The least powerful planet in the horoscope.

According to this author, death may occur in the Dasas and Bhukthis of the following planets which we are tabulating for the information of the reader.

Dasa or Period	Bhukthi or sub period
(1) Lord of the 8th	Lord of the 8th
(2) Lord of the 6th	Lord of the 8th
(3) Lord of the 8th	Malefic in the 6th
(4) Lord of the 6th	Planet in the 8th
(5) Lord of the 8th	Planets in association with the 6th lord planets aspected by the 8th lord.

(6)	A Malefic occupant of the 8th	The 6th lord
(7)	A Malefic occupant of the 6th	The 8th lord
(8)	A Malefic occupant of the 6th	8th lord occupying the 8th
(9)	A Malefic occupant of the 8th	A malefic occupant of the 6th

बुधशुक्रौ पचमस्थावन्योन्यौ मारकौ स्मृतौ ।
बुधदाये तु शुक्रस्तु शुक्रदाये बुधस्तथा ॥ १५ ॥

Stanza 15. If Mercury and Venus are in the 5th house, they become mutual Marakas.

NOTES

If Mercury and Venus are together in the 5th then death may occur in the Bhukthi of Mercury within the Dasa of Venus and vice versa. The combination is vague and it naturally implies that when these two planets are in the 5th and if according to the usual rules of maraka determination Mercury becomes a Maraka in his Dasa, then Venus will cause death in his *Bhukthi*, Venus becomes a maraka in his Dasa Buda kills the native in his bhukthi.

क्रूराधिपत्य युक्तस्तु कुजः पचमगो यदि ।
कुजदाये तु संप्राप्ते करोति निधनं कुजः ॥ १६ ॥

Stanza 16. Mars causes death in his own Dasa if he has evil lordship and is placed in the 5th house.

NOTES

Evil lordship means owning the 6th, 8th and 12th

houses. This can happen only when the Ascendant is Aries, Taurus, Virgo, Scorpio and Sagittarius. Mars should not only own either the 6th, the 8th, or the 12th house but should also be placed in the 5th to cause death in his Dasa.

अधिकाराच्छुभो मन्दो मारकग्रह संयुतः ।
अतीव बलवान्मृत्यो मारक प्रबलस्मृतः ॥ १७ ॥

Stanza 17. Even though Saturn may own favourable houses, he becomes powerful in causing death by being in conjunction with other marakas.

NOTES

Saturn is Ayushkaraka and the power to kill devolves on him if he joins death-inflicting planets. The good influences contributed by his favourable ownership cannot minimize Saturn's power to cause death. Saturn becomes favourable by virtue of owning a kendra or an angle and by owning both a Kendra and thrikona together which is possible in case of Taurus and Libra Ascendants.

लग्नस्थ रन्ध्रनाथस्य दशाकाले तु मारकः ।
रन्ध्रेश एव भवतीत्याहुज्ज्ञातक कोविदः ॥ १८ ॥

Stanza 18. Astrologers opine that death will be caused in the Dasa of the lord of the 8th who occupies the Ascendants.

द्वयेत्रयाणां पुत्राणां संप्राप्ते राहुदायके ।
पितुर्निधनमित्याहुस्तद्दशामध्य एव च ॥ १९ ॥

Stanza 19. If two or three sons of the native undergo Rahu Dasa simultaneously, then the person will die in his Dasa. And he will enjoy ordinary results.

NOTES

Stanza 18 is clear and requires no explanation. According to stanza 19, death of the person will happen in Rahu Dasa of his 2 or 3 sons—if they are to enjoy the said period simultaneously.

Thus ends the Tenth Chapter entitled "Combinations for Death" in Bhavartha Ratnakara of Sri Ramanujacharya.

Chapter 11

अथ महादशाफलतरङ्ग
Results of Dasas

शुक्रान्तरे शनेर्द्दाये शुक्रदाये तथा शने ।
अन्तर्द्दशायां संप्राप्ते योगहीनो भवेन्नरः ॥ १ ॥

Stanza 1. The person becomes unfortunate during Saturn's Dasa Venus Bhukthi or Venus Dasa, Saturn's Bhukthi.

शनिर्दाये तु शुक्रस्तु शुक्रदाये शनिस्तथा ।
मीने धनुषि जातस्य योगदो भवति ध्रुवम् ॥ २ ॥

Stanza 2. For persons born in Sagittarius and Pisces Ascendants, Venus and Saurn gives rise to Yoga in the Dasas of Saturn and Venus respectively.

NOTES

As we have already said elsewhere Yoga means affluence and fortunate results in general. One becomes devoid of affluence in Saturn's sub period in the major period of Venus and in the sub period of Venus within the Dasa of Saturn. This cannot be accepted as a rule or principle. There are several exceptions. Why Saturn should always produce evil results in the Dasa of Venus and vice versa ? In actual practice instance have come to our notice wherein Venus has produced affluence and riches in the Dasa of Saturn and vice versa. The following horoscope will illustrate our point.

Chart No.50—*Born on 7-8-1887 at about 1-30 p.m. (L.M.T.) Lat. 11° N.; Long. 77° 22' E.*

Moon			Mars	Rahu		Mars	
	Chart No. 50 RASI HJH-53		Sun Merc. Rahu Saturn	Sun Venus	NAVAMSA		Moon
Kethu							
	Ascdt.	Jupit.	Venus	Jupit.	Ascdt.	Merc.	Kethu Saturn

Balance of Jupiter's Dasa at birth : years 0-7-6.

In this horoscope Ascendant is Scorpio Saturn is lord of 3rd and 4th and occupies the 9th while Venus as lord of 7th and 12th occupies the 11th Saturn and Venus are disposed in the 3rd and 11th from each other. In the Navamsa the situation of Venus is favourable. Hence this sub period of Saturn in the major period of Venus did not cause any harm to the native. On the other hand, he enjoyed the sub period with beneficial results. Though stanza 1 says that the sub period of Venus in the Dasa of Saturn and that of Saturn in the Dasa of

Venus would produce injurious results due consideration must be shown to the general strength of these two planets in a horoscope.

The combination given in stanza 2 is however an exception to the one suggested in stanza 1 in as much as the principle that Saturn and Venus give rise to evil results in the Dasa of Venus and Saturn respectively should not be applied to persons, born in Pisces

Results of Dasas 147

and Sagittarius Ascendants. For Pisces Ascendants, Saturn owns the 11th and 12the houses and Venus rules over the 3rd and 8th. Thus both are malefic and probably on account of similar disposition in reference to Pisces Ascendants, their evil disposition may get counteracted and they be enabled to give rise to favourbale results.

षष्ठाष्टमव्ययस्थ रन्ध्रेशस्य ह्यतिर्यदा ।
षष्ठाष्टमव्ययेशानां भुक्तिकालो हि मारकः ॥ ३ ॥

Stanza 3. Death may be caused by the lords of the 6th, 8th and 12th houses in the course of the Dasa of the 8th lord who occupies the 6th 8th or 12th.

राज्यविक्रमपत्योश्च संबंधो यदि विद्यते ।
राज्येशदाये च योगस्सुयोगो विक्रमेशतुः ॥ ४ ॥

Stanza 4. If the lords of the 10th and the 3rd are in conjunction with or aspect each other the native will be deprived of fortune in the Dasa of the 10th lord and he will enjoy fortunate results in the Dasa of the 3rd lord.

NOTES

The third lordship is bad for any planet whereas a benefic owning the 10th becomes a temporary malefic while a malefic owning the 10th becomes temporarily benefic. When the 3rd and 10th lords join together then the 3rd lord gets the power to bestow fortunate results.

अपत्य भार्यं। भाग्येशाः निजराशिसु संस्थिताः ।
तद्दशान्तर्दशा प्राप्ते गंगस्नानं समश्नुते ॥ ५ ॥

Stanza 5. If the 5th, 7th and 9th lords are in their own houses they give rise to dips in Ganges during their periods and sub-periods.

सप्तमस्थ विलग्नस्य दाये स्वार्जित भाग्यभाक् ।
दारास्थ भाग्यराशीशदाये स्वार्जित भाग्यभाक् ॥ ६ ॥

Stanza 6. A person gets wealth by his own exertions in the Dasa of a planet occupying Ascendant or the 7th house. He will also acquire much wealth by his own efforts in the Dasa of the 9th lord occupying the 7th house.

NOTES

There is a lot of difference between inheriting ancestral wealth and property and acquiring the same by dint of his own efforts. There are periods when in spite of our best efforts we cannot acquire any wealth. One's exertions in the matter of getting wealth will meet with success (*a*) in the Dasa of planet occupying the 7th house, (*b*) in the Dasa of planet placed in the Ascendant and (*c*) in the Dasa of the 9th lord who occupies the 7th house.

राहुद्रदशायां संप्राप्ते राहुकेतोस्तथा शनेः ।
रवेरन्तर्भुक्तिकाले पिता मरणमाप्नुयात् ॥ ७ ॥

Stanza 7. The native's father will die in the sub-period of Rahu, Kethu, Saturn or the Sun within the Dasa of Rahu.

केतुद्रदशायां संप्राप्तो पितुमरणमुच्यते ।
भौममन्दरवीणां च राहोरन्तद्रदशासु च ॥ ८ ॥

Stanza 8. Father's death may be predicted in the sub-period of Mars, Saturn, the Sun or Rahu in the Dasa of Kethu.

धरासूनुर्दशाकाले पितुर्निधनमुच्यते ।
राहूकेतुशनीनां च रवेन्तर्दशासु हि ॥ ९ ॥

Results of Dasas

Stanza 9. Father's death will happen in the sub-periods of Rahu, Kethu, Saturn or the Sun in the Dasa of Mars.

शनेर्महद्द्दशाकाले पितुर्निधनमुच्यते ।
राहुभौमरवीणां च केतोरन्तर्दशासु हि ॥ १० ॥

Stanza 10. Father will die in the sub-period of Rahu, Mars, the Sun or Kethu in the Dasa of Saturn.

राहोर्महर्दशाकालात्पूर्वन्तु निधनं पितुः ।
धरासूनुर्दशाच्छिद्रकाले भवित निश्चयः ॥ ११ ॥

Stanza 11. Father's death will certainly happen just before the end of Mar's Dasa and the beginning of Rahu Dasa.

क्रूरग्रहर्दशाकाले राहोरन्तर्दशा यदा ।
तथैव निधनं बूयुः पितुर्जातक कोविदाः ॥ १२ ॥

Stanza 12. Astrologers say that one's father will die in the sub-period of Rahu in the Dasa of a malefic planet.

NOTES

Stanzas 7 to 12 inclusive deal with the periods which cause death to father. It will be seen that the various combinations mentioned in the above stanzas do not take into account the ownership of a planet but only their natural or Naisargika classification of malefics. Thus father's death is to happen in the sub period of any malefic planet within the major period of any malefic.

The ending of a Dasa goes under the technical name of *Dasachidra* and it is generally supposed to produce evil results. According to stanza 11, death of father will happen just before the ending of Mars Dasa and the beginning of Rahu Dasa. This may be taken to mean that in Mars Dasa when the sub period of a malefic is current, viz Kethu or the Sun, the father may die.

गुरूशुक्रौ वृश्चिकस्थौ शुक्रदाये समागमे ।
राजयोगकरश्शुक्रो भवेदेव न संशयः ॥ १३ ॥

Stanza 13. Venus confers Raja Yoga in his Dasa if he is in conjunction with Jupiter in Scorpio.

रवेस्सोमसुतस्यापि संबन्धे यदि विद्यते ।
बुधदाये प्रबलदो रवे दायस्थु मध्यमः ॥ १४ ॥

Stanza 14. When the Sun and Mercury are in conjunction with or aspect each other highly favourable results will be caused in the Dasa of Budha while Sun's Dasa will be ordinary.

चन्द्रमंगळ संबन्धे चन्द्रदाये बहुप्रदः ।
कुजदाये तु संप्राप्ते कुजदायस्तु मध्यमः ॥ १५ ॥

Stanza 15. When the Moon and Mars are in conjunction or aspect each other, fortunate result will be experienced in the Moon's Dasa while the Dasa of Mars will be quite ordinary.

गुरूशन्योश्च संबन्धे शनिदायो विशेषदः ।
गुरूदाये च संप्रोप्ते तद्दशा मध्यमास्मृता ॥ १६ ॥

Stanza 16. When Jupiter and Saturn join together or aspect each other Saturn Dasa will prove very fortunate while Jupiter's Dasa will be ordinary.

गुरोर ारकस्यापि संबन्धे यदि विद्यते ।
भौमदायास्तूत्तमस्याद् गुरूदायस्तु मध्यमः ॥ १७ ॥

Stanza 17. When Jupiter and Mars are in conjunction or aspect each other, Mars Dasa will be very fortunate and Jupiter's Dasa will be ordinary.

गुरोस्सुधांशु संबन्धे चन्द्रदायो विशेषदः ।
गुरोर्दशा संप्राप्तौ गुरूदायस्तु मध्यमः ॥ १८ ॥

Stanza 18. When Jupiter and the Moon join together, Moon Dasa will prove highly prosperous while Jupiter's Dasa will be ordinary.

NOTES

Stanzas 13 to 18 give interesting combinations to enable us to predict the relative good and bad nature of the results of Dasas of different planets in conjunction or mutual aspect. These combinations can be summarized as follows for the convenience of our esteemed readers.

Two planets in conjunction or in mutual aspect	Dasa in which highly benefic results will happen	Dasa in which ordinary results will happen
1. Venus and Jupiter in Conjunction in Scorpio	Venus	...
2. The Sun and Mercury	Mercury	The Sun
3. The Moon and Mars	Moon	Mars
4. Jupiter and Saturn	Saturn	Jupiter
5. Jupiter and Mars	Mars	Jupiter
6. Jupiter and Moon	Moon	Jupiter

It will be seen from the above that Jupiter is to produce only ordinary results in any of his combinations with Mars, the Moon and Saturn. This is however a general principle and its stands to be modified if Jupiter becomes a Yogakaraka or has some special distinction by way of exaltation or situation in Ascendant or the 10th or the 2nd or the 11th or the 9th house. The above tabulation will also enable us to anticipate that in the course of the dasa of the planets which are supposed to give ordinary results beneficial results will happen within the sub-periods of those whose major periods are supposed to prove highly fortunate. Thus if you take Jupiter and Saturn, then Saturn's bhukthi in Jupiter's Dasa will be highly fortunate.

Chart No.51—*Born on 8-8-1912 at about 7-23 p.m. (L.M.T.) Lat. 13° N.; Long. 77° 35' E.*

Rahu		Saturn Moon			Saturn	Venus	
Ascdt.	Chart No. 51 RASI		Sun	Sun Rahu	NAVAMSA		Moon Merc. Kethu
			Mars Merc. Venus	Ascdt.			
	Jupit.		Kethu		Jupit.	Mars	

Balance of Mars' Dasa at birth : years 6-0-10.

In Chart No. 51, it will be seen that (*a*) Jupiter and Saturn aspect each other (*b*) Mars aspects Jupiter (*c*) and Jupiter and Moon aspect each other. Consequently Saturn's Dasa will be much more beneficial than Jupiter's. The native will not enjoy the Dasas of the Moon and Mars. The sub period of the Moon Mars and Saturn will also prove much more beneficial

Results of Dasas

than the sub periods of other planets in Jupiter Dasa. Here we have not taken into account the strength or weakness, of any of these planets. Jupiter's Dasa Jupiter bhukthi proved very unfortunate to the native as Jupiter is in Scorpio in the 10th house, whereas the fortunes were considerably advanced in the bhukthi of Saturn. Saturn is lord of Ascendant and he is in the 4th in a friendly sign aspected by Jupiter lord of the 2nd. Moreover for Lunar Ascendant, Saturn becomes a Yogakaraka and his situation in Lunar Ascendant aspected by Jupiter enables him to give much more favourable and fortunate results than Jupiter.

The combinations of Moon and Mars, Jupiter and Mars, and Jupiter and Moon go under the special distinction of *Moon mangala Yoga Jupiter mangala Yoga* and *Gaja kesari Yoga* respectively and out of the two planets causing each Yoga, one become capable of producing much more favourable results than the other. It will be seen that only ordinary results will happen in the Dasa of the other planet and not unfortunate results.

केन्द्रकोणस्थ राहोश्च दायकाले समागमे ।
स्वतन्त्र राजयोगं च महत्कीर्तिं समश्नुते ॥ १९ ॥

Stanza 19. Rahu will confer Raja Yoga and much fame in his Dasa if he joins a quadrant or a trine.

गुरोर्बुधस्य शुक्रस्य संबन्धो यदि विद्यते ।
विशेष धनयोगश्च कीर्तिमान्भाग्यवान् भवेत् ॥ २० ॥

Stanza 20. If Jupiter, Mercury and Venus join together or are in mutual aspect the native becomes very wealthy famous and fortunate.

शुक्रस्य यदि संबन्धो बुधेन गुरूणापि वा ।
शुक्रदाये च संप्राप्ते धनयोगं लभेन्नरः ॥ २१ ॥

Stanza 21. The native will earn which wealth in Venus' Dasa if Venus is in conjunction with or aspected by Mercury or Jupiter.

गुरूदाये च संप्राप्ते धनहीनो भनेन्नरः ।
बुधस्यदाये संप्राप्ते मिश्रयोगो भवेद ध्रुवम् ॥ २२ ॥

Stanza 22. The native becomes bereft of wealth in the Dasa of Jupiter and mixed results will be produced in the Dasa of Mercury, when the said planets are disposed as per stanza 21.

NOTES

Rahu when occupying a Kendra (quadrant) or Trikona (trine) is supposed to give rise to Raja Yoga in his Dasa.

If Jupiter Mercury and Venus are in mutual conjunction, or aspect, one becomes fortunate and wealthy. All these three planets are benefics (Mercury becomes benefic here as he will be with the other two benefics) but only one of the three in combination can really enable the native to acquire wealth in his, Dasa Stanza 22 makes the meaning very clear. If Venus is in conjunction with or aspected by Mercury or Jupiter then.

(a) Venus confers wealth in his Dasa.

(b) Jupiter causes loss of wealth in his Dasa, and

(c) Mercury produces mixed results in his Dasa

Remember that for each of these three planets to produce the results ascribed above they must conjoin together or aspect each other. If Venus and Jupiter make up the combination the latter gives evil results and if Venus and Mercury cause the combination, the latter produces mixed results.

रव्यादि ग्रहयोगसंयोगे रवेर्दाये समागमे ।
रविर्योगदोयुक्तः इतरे मध्यमास्मृताः ॥ २३ ॥

Stanza 23. If the Sun and other planets combine together, the Sun confer fame and wealth in his Dasa while the other planets give ordinary results.

ग्रहैरन्यैश्च राहोस्तु संबन्धो यदि विद्यते ।
यो ग्रहः प्रबलस्तेषां तत्फलं च ददाति सः ॥ २४ ॥

Stanza 24. Of the several planets who are in conjunction with or aspected by Rahu, the strongest one gives the results indicated by it.

राहुसूर्यस्तथामन्दस्तु तृतीये यदि संस्थितः ।
राहोर्दशा विपाकस्तु भाग्य विक्रमयोगदः ॥ २५ ॥

Stanza 25. When Rahu, the Sun and Saturn are in the 3rd, Rahu gives rise to courage and fortune in his Dasa.

राहोर्दशा विपाकेतु विक्रमस्थो बुधोयदि ।
धैर्यहीनो भवेज्जात इति जातककोविदाः ॥ २६ ॥

Stanza 26. Astrologers say that during the Dasa of Rahu one becomes timed if Mercury is in the 3rd house.

NOTES

If planets are in conjunction with the Sun, they become astangata or combust. Combustion occurs when the planets are very near the Sun. Otherwise it cannot be called combustion. If the Sun and other planets join together, the Sun confers fame and fortune in his Dasa while ordinary results will be given by other planets. Stanzas 24 requires some explanation. For example Jupiter, Venus and Saturn are in conjunction with Rahu. Of these three let us assume that Jupiter is the most powerful and he owns the 5th house, and occupies the 9th house. Then Jupiter alone will be able to produce in his Dasa results of his indication viz, children and fortune. The indications of the other two planets become more or less defunct. The original stanza say, *Rahasthusambandho*—meaning both conjunction and aspect. Of the several planets aspecting Rahu the results indicated by that which is most powerful will manifest in the course of his Dasa in preference to the others.

Chart No.52—*Born on 8-8-1912 at about 7-23 p.m. (L.M.T.) Lat. 13° N.; Long. 77° 35' E.*

Rahu		Saturn Moon			Saturn	Venus	
Ascdt.	Chart No. 52 RASI		Sun	Sun Rahu	NAVAMSA		Moon Merc. Kethu
			Mars Merc. Venus	Ascdt.			
	Jupit.		Kethu		Jupit.	Mars	

Balance of Mars' Dasa at birth : years 6-0-10.

In *Chart No. 52* Rahu is aspected by Mars and Jupiter. The latter is more powerful. Therefore the indications of Jupiter—finance, professional prospects and gain will manifest in the course of Jupiter's Dasa.

Rahu, the Sun and Saturn are all first rate malefics. Still if these three are together in the 3rd, Rahu can cause Yoga in his Dasa.

Thus ends the Eleventh Chapter entitled 'Results of Dasas' in Bhavartha Ratnakara of Sri Ramanujacharya.

Chapter 12

अथ ग्रहसामान्ययोगतरङ्ग
Ordinary Combinations

तत्तद्भावेश्वराः खवेटाः तत्तत्कारक संयताः ।
तस्य भावस्य सर्वस्य प्राबल्यं प्रोच्यते बुधैः ॥ १ ॥

Stanza 1. The learned in astrology say that all such bhavas whose lords are in conjunction with the respective karakas become strong.

NOTES

Each Bhava comprehends several significations. If a bhava is strongly disposed all its significations will fully manifest. A bhava gets vitality if its lor joins its karaka. Each bhava has its own karaka, *viz*, the Sun is the karaka for Ascendant and the 9th (father), the Moon is the karaka of the 4th (mother), Mars is the karaka of the 3rd (brothers), Jupiter is the karaka of the 2nd (wealth) and 5th (children), Venus is the karaka of the 7th (wife or husband), Saturn is the karaka of the 8th or Longevity. Thus the Ascendant bhava gains strength if its lord joins the Ascendant karaka, *viz*, the Sun, similarly the 4th Bhava gains vitality if the 4th lord is with the Moon, the karaka for the 4th house.

तृतीयाष्टमलाभाधिपतित्वन्तु स दोषकम् ।
सुतभाग्याधिपत्यन्तु खेटानां शुभदं भवेत् ॥ २ ॥

Stanza 2. Lords of the 3rd, 8th and 11th produce evil. Lords of the 5th and 9th give good results.

NOTES

In *Jathakachandrika* which is more or less an epitome of Parasara's work, the ownership of the 3rd, 6th and 11th has been considered as productive of evil while here, reference has been made to the lordship of the 8th. I have to observe that the 8th lordship is not as malefic as that of the 6th.

तथापि च गुरोराशिद्धातृ षष्ठाष्टमेशितः ।
रन्ध्रस्थान स्थितश्चापि योगदा भवति ध्रुवम् ॥ ३ ॥

Stanza 3. Even Jupiter becomes evil by owning the 3rd, 6th and 8th. However, in spite of owning the 8th he will confer fame and wealth.

NOTES

An important principle is enumerated in this stanza Jupiter becomes a malefic as lord of the 3rd, 6th or 8th but his power to confer Yoga will not be obstructed even if he owns the 8th. This means that in his Dasa, he will confer fame name and wealth but on account of the stigma due to this ownership, he may give rise to malefic results as sub lord in his Dasa or in that of other planets.

शुक्रस्य षष्ठसंस्थानं योगदं भवति ध्रुवम् ।
व्ययस्थितस्य शुक्रस्य यथा योगं वदन्ति हि ॥ ४ ॥

Stanza 4. Venus in the 6th will certainly give rise to fame and affluence. He will give the same results in the 12th house also.

राज्यलाभ चतुर्थेषु पचमे वा स्थितो यदि ।
राहुर्येगप्रदःप्रोक्तो विद्वद्भिर्जातक कोविदैः ॥ ५ ॥

Stanza 5. Astrologers say that fame and affluence are conferred if Rahu is in the 10th, 11th, 4th and 5th houses.

केन्द्राधिपति यस्सौम्य खेटायदि नयोगदाः ।
केन्द्रस्था केन्द्रनाथस्तु क्रूरश्चेद्राजयोगदाः ॥ ६ ॥

Stanza 6. Benefics become evil by owning Kendra Malefic planets produce Raja Yoga by owning or occupying kendras.

NOTES

We are coming to the general principles of astrology Venus becomes beneficial in the 6th and 12th houses. Rahu gives rise to Yoga by occupying the 10th, 11th, 4th and 5th houses. For natural benefics such as Jupiter, Venus and well associated Mercury lordship of kendras or quadrants is not desirable. Natural malefics, viz., the Mars, Saturn, Sun and badly associated Mercury may even cause Raja Yoga by owning or occupying kendras. Prof. B. S. Rao used to tell me that a natural malefic cannot become a Yogakaraka by the mere fact of owning a Kendra. At best he will lose his evil nature. The notes given to stanza 6 of *Jathaka Chandrika* by Prof. B.S. Rao in his English translation are very illuminating and deals exhaustively with the question of malefics and benefics owning kendras.

यस्मिन् भावे स्थितो मन्दो य भावं वीक्षितेथवा ।
तस्य तस्यापि भावस्यन्यूनतां च वदन्ति हि ॥ ७ ॥

Stanza 7. The house which is occupied or aspected by Saturn becomes defective.

NOTES

This is a very important combination and is full of significance Saturn destroys the indications of the bhava in which he is situated except the 8th house. If he is in the 2nd, you will see that the native will never save any money in spite of big earnings. He will die a pauper or in very adverse financial circumstances. Of course there are exceptions to this rule when Saturn is a Yoga karaka. When Saturn is in the 10th house he will not destroy the indication On the contrary, he gives fame, name, leadership and the like. But he gives the subject a sudden fall. The next stanza gives certain exceptions to the general principle enunciated in stanza 7.

विक्रमं भाग्यराशिश्च शनिना वीक्षितो यदि ।
तस्य भावस्य प्राबल्यमित्यूचुर्गणकोत्तमाः ॥ ८ ॥

Stanza 8. If Saturn aspects the 3rd and 9th houses, the will gain strength.

क्षीणचन्द्रो विलग्नस्थो मन्दधीरन्यपोषितः ।
पूर्णचन्द्रो विलग्नस्थो गुणवान् धनवान् भवेत् ॥ ९ ॥

Stanza 9. Weak (waning) Moon in Ascendant makes the native dull and dependent. He will become rich and a man of character if the waxing Moon is in the Ascendant.

विलग्नस्थौ चन्द्रभौमौ वा मूर्ति भाग्यवान् भवेत् ।
चतुर्थेशयुतो भौमः क्षेत्रवान् भवति ध्रुवम् ॥ १० ॥

Stanza 10. The native becomes fortunate if the Moon and Mars are either in Ascendant or the 8th house. He acquires houses if Mars joins the 4th lord.

NOTES

According to stanza 10, *Chandra Mangala Yoga* occurring in Ascendant or in the 8th is good. Mars by himself is not good in the 8th as he will kill the wife (or husband) early in life. But Mars when he is with the Moon in the 8th loses his evil nature so that the general fortune of the native is promoted.

Mars is the karaka for lands and the 4th house rules houses and landed properties. When Mars is in conjunction with the lord of the 4th, the native acquires landed properties and houses.

Chart No. 53—*Born on 8-8-1912 at about 7-23 p.m. (L.M.T.) Lat. 13° N.; Long. 77° 35' E.*

Rahu		Saturn Moon			Saturn	Venus	
Ascdt.	Chart No. 53 RASI		Sun	Sun Rahu	NAVAMSA		
			Mars Merc. Venus	Ascdt.			Moon Merc. Kethu
	Jupit.		Kethu		Jupit.	Mars	

Balance of Mars' Dasa at birth : years 6-0-10.

In *Chart No. 53* lord of the 4th is in the 7th with Mars. This is indicative of the subject getting access to house properties. The planet owning, occupying or aspecting the 4th or the planet who is in conjunction with the 4th lord will give house property in his Dasa or Bhukthi. In the example horoscope, the native purchased a house in Jupiter's Dasa (Jupiter aspecting 4th and occupying the house of Mars) Mercury's

Bhukthi. Mercury is in conjunction with not only the 4th lord but also Mars.

चतुर्थनाथ देवेज्यौ य चतुर्थे यदि संस्थितौ ।
चतुष्पाद वृद्धियोगो यमित्याहुर्जातककोविदाः ॥ ११ ॥

Stanza 11. The person acquires cattle and other domestic animals if Jupiter is in the 4th house with the lord of the 4th.

पापमध्यगता भावास्तथा भावेशकारकाः ।
तद्भाव भावराशीश कारका दुःखदायकाः ॥ १२ ॥

Stanza 12. Any house or its lord or its karaka if hemmed in between malefics will produce evil results.

लाभव्ययधिपत्योश्च संबन्धो योगदो भवेत् ।
लाभाधिपस्तृतीये वा व्यये वा योगदो भवेत् ॥ १३ ॥

Stanza 13. If the lords of the 11th and 12th join together or aspect each other, they produce good results. And the 11th lord, produces good results if he occupies the 3rd or 12th house.

सर्व राशिषु जातस्य भाग्येशोऽष्टमे यदि ।
न योगं लभते जात सामान्यो भवति ध्रुवम् ॥ १४ ॥

Stanza 14. For persons born in any Ascendant, the presence of the lord of the 9th in the 8th does not give rise to any Yoga—but only ordinary results will be produced.

षष्ठस्थो यदि वा चन्द्रो वृद्धिकौशल्यवान् भवेत् ।
द्वितीयस्थो भवेच्चन्द्रः नेत्र चचलवान् भवेत् ॥ १५ ॥

Stanza 15. The Moon in the 6th makes the native intelligent. He will be fickle minded if the Moon is in the 3rd.

Stanza 16. Astrologers say that beginning from Aries the zodiacal signs are odd and even.

NOTES

Three elements make up a Bhava and they are the Bhava (house) Bhavadhipathi (lord of the house) and Bhavakakarka (indicator of the house). These three factors should not be hemmed in between malefics. If all the three factors have malefics on either side then, the vitality of the Bhava will be so weak, that it stands self-condemned. If however any one of the factors is subject to the presence of malefics on either side, the prospects of the Bhava in question will be fairly good. If two of the elements are subject to this affliction, the strength of the Bhava would indeed be ordinary.

The combination given in stanza 13 that if the 11th and 12th lords combine together or aspect each other, is important and it will be found to be applicable in a large majority of cases.

Chart No. 54—*Born on 8-8-1912 at about 7-23 p.m. (L.M.T.) Lat. 13° N.; Long. 77° 35' E.*

Rahu	Saturn Moon			Rahu	Saturn	Venus	
Ascdt.	Chart No. 54 RASI		Sun	Ascdt.	NAVAMSA		Sun
			Mars Merc. Venus				Mars Merc. Venus
	Jupit.		Kethu		Jupit.		Kethu

Balance of Mars' Dasa at birth : years 6-0-10.

Ordinary Combination

In this *Chart No. 54* lords of the 11th and 12th are Jupiter and Saturn respectively. Note they are in mutual aspect and this has given rise to an important Yoga or special combination.

The dictum that the fortunes will be ordinary if the 9th lord is in the 8th (vide stanza 14) can hold good provided the 9th Bhava is also weak. Otherwise this combination should be applied very cautiously.

The 16th stanza needs no explanation as it deals with the fundamentals of astrology. Aries is an odd sign. Taurus is even. Gemini is odd. Cancer is even and so on.

Thus, ends the 12th Chapter entitled "Ordinary Combinations" in Bhavartha Ratnakara of Sri Ramanujacharya.

Chapter 13

अथ ग्रहमालिकयोगाः
Graha Malika Yogas

लग्नादिवाणसंख्याक राशिगा नवखचेरा ।
स्थिताश्चेत्पच खेटास्य मालिका योग उच्चेत ॥ १ ॥

Stanza 1. If all the nine planets occupy the five houses from Ascendants, *Panchagraha malika Yoga* is caused.

NOTES

The chapter is headed *Graha MalikaYoga*. In Sanskrit *Malika* means garland or a wreath of flowers and *Gral amalika* means a wreath of planets. In standard works on astrology, Malika Yoga is defined as the disposition of the seven planets in seven houses contiguously. If the planets are disposed from Ascendant, it is Ascendant malika Yoga, if they are disposed from the 2nd, it is Dhana malika and so on. When the seven signs beginning from any particular sign are occupied by the seven planets, a semi circle is formed and the term *Malika* will more or less be justified.

The author of this work takes into account the nine planets (which obviously include Rahu and Kethu) and the disposition of the 9 planets from Ascendant within a certain number of signs is said to give rise to the different types of Malika. Readers should therefore note that according to our author the malika or garland should commence only from Ascendant while according to other standard works, the mala can commence from any house. Another important difference is, that according to the general principles of astrology the seven planets should occupy the seven houses beginning from any house whereas this author suggests that the nine planets should be disposed within five to nine houses from Ascendant.

Chart No. 55—*Born on 5-10-1942 at about 10-17 p.m. (I.S.T.) Lat. 13° N.; Long. 77° 35' E.*

		Ascdt. Saturn		Venus			Mars
Kethu	Chart No. 55 RASI 3-121		Jupit. Moon	Moon	NAVAMSA		Jupit. Sun Saturn Rahu
			Rahu	Kethu			
		Merc.	Sun Mars Venus			Merc.	Ascdt.

Balance of Mercury's Dasa at birth : years 4-7-2.

Stanza 1. Says that *Panchagrahmalika* Yoga is caused if all the nine planets occupy the first five houses. This should not be confused with the *PasaYoga* mentioned by Varahamihira when dealing with the 32 Nabhasa Yogas. When all planets occupy *any five signs* PasaYoga is caused. Note the distinction between *any five signs* and within the *first five signs*.

A little reflection will show to the reader that *all the nine planets* can never occupy the first five houses because Kethu is always to be in the 7th from Rahu. Either the combination is impossible or it should mean that eight planets should occupy the five houses from Ascendant. I am inclined to think that the author must have been aware of this error which is discernible even to an elementary student. Why, having known that nine planets cannot occupy the first five or six houses he has still mentioned the combination. I cannot explain.

Chart No. 56—*Born on 28/29-8-1898 at about 5-33 a.m. (L.M.T.) Lat. 16° 50′ N.; Long. 5h .3m. E.*

			Mars Kethu		Moon	Kethu	Jupit.
	Chart No. 56 RASI 3-121				NAVAMSA		Ascdt.
Moon			Sun Ascdt. Merc.				Sun
Rahu	Saturn		Jupit. Venus	Merc.	Rahu Mars Saturn		Venus

Balance of Moon's Dasa at birth : years 9-8-12.

Chart No. 55 is an illustration of the *Panchagraha malika Yoga*, in as much as all the eight planets are in the first five signs from Ascendant.

Chart No. 56 illustrates *Pasa Yoga* in as much as all the seven planets are disposed in five houses.

लग्नमारभ्यये खेटाः ऋतु संख्य सुराशिषु ।
स्थिताश्चेत्षष्ठ खेटाख्यामालिका योग उच्यते ॥ २ ॥

Stanza 2. If all the planets occupy six houses from Ascendant *Shashtagraha malika* Yoga is caused.

NOTES

As I have already pointed out all the nine planets cannot occupy the 1st six houses—only eight can occupy. It is also clear that all the houses (from 1 to 5,6,7,8 or 9) should be occupied and no one house should be vacant, to cause Malika Yoga.

लग्नामारभ्य शैलाख्य संख्य राशिषु खेचराः ।
स्थितश्चेत्सप्तखेटाख्या मालिका योग उच्यते ॥ ३ ॥

Stanza 3. If all the planets occupy the seven houses from Ascendant, *Sapthagraha malika Yoga* is caused.

लग्नामारभ्यवस्वाख्यराशिस्था खेचरा यदि ।
अष्टखेचरमालाख्य योगप्रोक्तस्तु सूरिभिः ॥ ४ ॥

Stanza 4. If all the planets occupy the eight houses from Ascendant, *Ashtagraha malika* Yoga is caused.

लग्नादारभ्य भागाख्य संख्यराशिषु खेचराः ।
स्थिताश्चेन्नव खेटाख्या मालिका योग उच्यते ॥ ५ ॥

Stanza 5. If all the planets occupy the nine houses from Ascendant *Navagraha malika* Yoga is caused.

केचिद्वदन्ति सूर्यादि ग्रहाणां क्रमशस्थितिः ।
मालिका ग्रहयोगो यमितिजातककोविदाः ॥ ६ ॥

Stanza 6. Some astrologers say that *Graha malika Yoga* commences from the Sun.

केचिद्वदन्ति लग्नाधिराशिषु क्रमशो ग्रहः ।
स्यिताश्चेद् ग्रहमालाख्य योगीयमिति कोविदाः ॥ ७ ॥

Stanza 7. And still others say that Malika Yoga commences from Ascendant.

NOTES

I have already explained in the notes given above that the generality of astrologers maintain that *Malika* can commence from Ascendant or any house—but seven houses should be occupied by the seven planets (excluding of course Rahu and Kethu). Here we take rather the author wants us to take into account, all the nine planets and for the first two Graham Malika Yogas involving 5 and 6 houses only eight planets can be taken. No where else it seems to have been said that the counting must be made from the Sun. Consequently reference to this suggestion made in stanza 6 may be easily ignored.

षष्ठ सप्ताष्ट नवभि संख्याख्याः ग्रहमालिकाः ।
भवन्ति यस्य जातस्य भाग्ययोगप्रदा स्मृताः ॥ ८ ॥

Stanza 8. A person born in the Graha Malika Yoga caused by the presence of planets in 6 7 8 or 9 houses from Ascendant will be fortunate.

पचखेटाख्यमालापि यस्य जातस्य विद्यते ।
भाग्योगस्तु वक्तव्यस्तस्य ज्योतिषकोत्तमैः ॥ ९ ॥

Stanza 9. Astrologers say that a person born in the *Graha Malika Yoga* caused by the presence of planets in the 5 houses from Ascendant will also be fortunate.

NOTES

In general all the five types of *Graha Malika Yoga* caused by the presence of the planets in the 5, 6, 7, 8 or 9 houses from Ascendant are said to make a person born in them fortunate. The term used by the author is *Bhagya Yoga*—which literally translated means fortunate combination. Before illustrating

Graha Malika Yogas

these Yogas I shall make a passing reference to some of the Nabhasa Yogas and also to the *Malika Yogas* as propounded in other standard astrological works.

I have already referred to *Pasa Yoga* and have given in example for it Pasa. Yoga means that all the seven planets should occupy any five signs and not the *first five houses*. One born in Pasa Yoga is said to be talkative clever in the acquisition of virtue and wealth and he will have sons.

If all the seven planets are in any 6 signs (in contra distinction to bhavas or houses) *Damani Yoga* is caused. This is also one of the *Nabhasa Yogas*. According to our author *Shashtagraha Malika Yoga* is caused if all the planets are in the six signs from the 1st house, Damini Yoga also produces favourbale results.

Chart No. 57—*Born on 7-6-1898 at about 1-35 p.m. (L.M.T.) Lat. 11° N.; Long. 5h. 8m. E.*

	Mars / Sun Merc.	Venus / Kethu	Merc. / Jupit.		Venus	Kethu / Mars
	Chart No. 57 RASI (Damini Yoga) 3-49		Moon	NAVAMSA		
Moon			Ascdt.			Sun
Rahu	Saturn	Jupit. Ascdt.	Rahu Saturn			

Balance of Sun's Dasa at birth : years 2-5-16.

Readers must able to appreciate the difference between *Damini Yoga* (*Chart No. 57*) and Shashta Malika Yoga (*Chart No. 58*). In Horoscope No. 57 it will be seen that all the planets (note Rahu and Kethu excepted) are posited in any *six signs* where as in

Chart No. 58 the eight planets are occupying the six signs from *Ascendants*.

Chart No. 58—*Born on 7-5-1861 at about 4-2 a.m. (L.M.T.) Lat. 22° 40' N.; Long. 88° 30' E.*

Ascdt. Moon	Sun Merc. Venus	Mars Kethu	Jupit. Ascdt.		Kethu	Merc.
	Chart No. 58 RASI Shashta Malika	Jupit.		NAVAMSA		Saturn
		Saturn	Moon			
Rahu				Venus Sun Rahu	Mars	

Balance of Mercury's Dasa at birth : years 9-5-22.

Chart No. 59—*Born on 10-5-1903 at Gh.27-30 after sunrise, Lat. 13° N.; Long. 77° 35' E.*

Kethu	Sun	Merc.	Venus			Jupit.	Saturn Merc.
Jupit.	Chart No. 59 RASI			Moon Mars	NAVAMSA		Rahu
Saturn				Kethu			
		Ascdt. Moon	Rahu Mars		Ascdt. Venus Sun		

Balance of Rahu's Dasa at birth : years 6-7-11.

Now we come to the *next Yoga*, viz *Sapthagraha Malika Yoga* which is supposed to be caused if all the nine planets occupy the *seven sings from Ascendant*. It has its counter part (note there is no comparison) in

Graha Malika Yogas

Vallaki Yoga one of the *Nabhasa Yogas*. If all planets occupy *any seven signs*, Vallaki is caused. The man born in Vallaki will be skilled and likes music and dancing.

In *Chart No. 59* it will be seen that the seven planets have occupied seven signs. Combinations given in stanzas 5 and 6 are easy to comprehend and they do not require any further explanation.

Satayoga Manjari (vide English Translation by B. Suryanarain Rao) gives a clear explanation of Malika Yoga as *also Jathaka Parijatha*. When all the seven planets occupy the seven houses from Ascendant, it is *Lagnamalika*, from the 2nd *Dhana Malika* and so on. Thus 12 different *Malika Yogas* are formed which I am giving (on next page) for the readers information.

There is one more point, which in its very nature is con-troversial and which I do not propose to deal with in these pages. And that is, whether in reckoning these Yogas, Bhavas should be considered or the Rasis. According to Varahamihira, Rasa, Kshetra, Griha, Riksha, Bha, Bhavana are all synonymous terms. But in common parlance Rasi means sign and Griha or Bhava means house. Our author uses specific word Rasi and therefore there seems to be no doubt that in the reckoning of Malika Yoga Rasis are meant and not bhavas.

For *Sankhya Yogas* the signs are considered where as houses are taken into account for *Yogas*. However I do not want the reader to confuse the issue. I have dealt with this subject in some of my articles in the columns of *The Astrological Magazine* and in my lates book *Three Hundred Important Combinations*.

	Name of Malika Yoga	Definition	Result
1.	Langamalika	All planets in the seven house from Lagna	King, Commander, wealthy
2.	Dhanamalika	All planets in the 2nd house from Lagna	Very wealthy, dutiful, resolute, unsympathetic
3.	Vikramamalika	All planets in the 3rd house from Lagna	Ruler, rich, sickly, surrounded by brave men
4.	Sukhamalika	All planets in the 4th house from Lagna	Charitable, liberal, wealthy
5.	Putramalika	All planets in the 5th house from Lagna	Highly religious and famous
6.	Satrumalika	All planets in the 6th house from Lagna	Greedy, somewhat poor
7.	Kalatramalika	All planets in the 7th house from Lagna	Coveted by women and influential
8.	Randhramalika	All planets in the 8th house from Lagna	Poor and hen-pecked
9.	Bhagyamalika	All planets in the 9th house from Lagna	Religious, well-to-do, mighty and good
10.	Karmamalika	All planets in the 10th house from Lagna	Respected, virtuous
11.	Labhamalika	All planets in the 11th house from Lagna	Skillful and lord of lovely women
12.	Vrayamalika	All planets in the 12th house from Lagna	Honoured, liberal and respected

Graha Malika Yogas

समाराशिस्थ खेटानां मूलकोणाधिपत्यजम् ।
फलमग्रे तु तदनुचेदितर राशीशतां फलम् ॥ १० ॥

Stanza 10. Planets occupying even signs produce results pertaining to their trinal ownership in the beginning the results due to the other ownership will be conferred afterwards.

ओजराशिस्थ खेटानामितराधीशतां फलत् ।
त्वग्रे भवति कोणाधिपत्यजं फलमन्यथा ॥ ११ ॥

Stanza 11. Planets occupying odd signs produce results pertaining to ownerships of Rasi etc., in the beginning, the results due to trinal lordships will be conferred afterwards.

NOTES

Take Saturn in *Chart No. 60*. He is in an even sign. He owns Ascendant and also the 12th. In his Dasa or in his Bhukthi, the results due to his ownership of Ascendant and the 12th house will be produced, not in

Chart No. 60—*Born on 8-8-1912 at about 7-23 p.m. (L.M.T.) Lat. 13° N.; Long. 77° 35' E.*

Rahu		Saturn Moon			Saturn	Venus	
Ascdt.	Chart No. 60 RASI		Sun	Sun Rahu	NAVAMSA		Moon Merc. Kethu
			Mars Merc. Venus	Ascdt.			
	Jupit.		Kethu		Jupit.	Mars	

Balance of Mercury's Dasa at birth : years 9-5-22.

the beginning of the Dasa or bhukthi but afterwards i.e., in the middle and concluding parts.

Take Venus. He is in an odd sign. He owns a Kendra (4th) and also a trikona. The results due to his Kendra ownership will happen in the beginning of his Dasa (*or bhukthi*) while the results due to his trinal ownership may be produced 'afterwards' *i.e.*, in the middle and last parts.

रवे: द्वितीयस्थ खगा शीघ्र:गाश्च भवन्ति हि ।
रवेस्तृतीयस्थ खगा समानगतयो भवत् ॥ १२ ॥

Stanza 12. A planet in the 2nd from the Sun possesses swift motion, the one in the 3rd from the Sun will have even motion.

रवेश्चतुर्थस्थ खगा: भवेयुर्मंदगामिन: ।
रवे:पचम षष्ठस्था: भवेयुर्वंक्रगास्सदा ॥ १३ ॥

Stanza 13. Planets in the 4th from the Sun possess slow motion, those in the 5th and 6th have somewhat retrograde motion.

रवेस्सप्तमरन्ध्रस्था ग्रहाश्चात्यन्त वक्रगा: ।
रवेसुधर्मकर्मस्था। ग्रहाणां कुटिलागति: ॥ १४ ॥

Stanza 14. Planets in the 7th and 8th from the Sun possess retrograde motion, those in the 9th and 10th from the Sun will have transverse motion.

रवेर्लाभ व्ययस्थाश्च ग्रहश्चात्यन्त शीघ्रगा: ।
शुभग्रहाणां शीघ्रगतयो बलहीनदा: ॥ १५ ॥

Stanza 15. Planets in the 11th and 12th from the Sun possess very swift motion. Swift motion renders benefics devoid of strength.

Graha Malika Yogas

क्रूरग्रहाणां वक्रगतयश्शुभर्योगदाः ।
इत्येवं हि ग्रहगतीद्रष्टव्या गणिकोत्तमैः ॥ १६ ॥

Stanza 16. Malefics cause good by having retrograde motion. In this way should be ascertained the movements of planets by the learned in mathematics.

NOTES

In the first five stanzas the author introduces some astronomical elements. For astrological purposes they could be taken to mean that planets, when situated at certain distances from the Sun become strong or weak and thereby capable of producing certain good or bad results.

In other words the above means that all planets produce ordinary results in the 3rd 5th 9th and 10th places from the Sun Malefics and benefics produce favaourable and adverse results respectively in 2, 5, 6, 7, 8, 11 and 12th places from the Sun.

This is of course the interpretation I have put. The author has briefly suggested the different kinds of motions of the planets and how they are beneficial or otherwise. According to *Suryasiddhanta* the motion of a planet is of eight kinds viz., *Vakra* (somewhat retrograde), *ativakra* (retrograde), *Kutila* (transverse), *Monda* (slow), *Atimanda* (very slow), *Sama* (even), *Seeghra* (swift) and *Astiseeghra* (very swift). We do not know the precise difference between the various kinds of motion as they have not been elaborated. Our author mention all the above kinds of motion except *Atimanda* (very slow) *Kutila* is held by some as a form of retrograde motion. According to others it is used to designate the motion of a planet when, being for the moment stationary in respect to longitude, and accordingly neither advancing nor retrograding, it is changing its latitude. The reader need not have to worry with these highly technical points which are of purely astronomical interest.

Thus ends the Thirteenth Chapter entitedl "MalikaYoga" in Bhavartha Ratnakara of Sri Ramanujacharya.

Chapter 14

अथ ग्रहाणां स्वक्षेत्रादि विचार तरङ्ग
Planetary Rulerships, etc.

THE SUN — अथ रवेः

उच्चस्थानं रवेर्मेषं वृषभे तु द्विषद्गृहम् ।
मिथुन तु समक्षेत्रं मित्रक्षेत्रकुळीरकम् ॥ १ ॥

Stanza 1. Aries is the place of exaltation for th Sun, Taurus is an inimical sign, Gemini is neutral, cancer is friendly.

स्वक्षेत्रं मूलकोणं च सिंहप्रोक्तस्तु सूरिभिः ।
कन्याभं तु समक्षेत्रं तुलानीचारि मन्दिरम् ॥ २ ॥

Stanza 2. For the Sun, Leo is Moolatrikona and own house, Virgo is neutral, Libra is the place of debilitation.

मित्रक्षेत्रे कीटधनुषी मकरं स्याद्द्विषद्गृहम् ।
कुम्भोपि शत्रुक्षेत्रच मित्रक्षेत्रस्तु मीनभम् ।
रवेर्गृहाणां गणनात्वेवं प्रोक्ताच सूरिभिः ॥ ३ ॥

Stanza 3. Scorpio and Sagittarius are friendly signs, Capricorn and Aquarius are inimical and Pisces friendly. So has to be ascertained the Sun's relationship with the signs.

NOTES

In the concluding part of the work, the author deals with elements of astrology. The friendly, neutral or inimical nature of a sign for the Sun is based on the friendly, neutral or inimical nature of the disposition of its lord. Thus as Venus is an enemy of the Sun, Taurus is an inimical sign.

THE MOON — अथ चन्द्र:

विधोरजा समक्षेत्रमुच्चस्थानं वृपस्तथा ।
मूलकोणं तथा प्रोक्तं मित्रक्षेत्रं तु युग्मभम् ॥ ४ ॥

Stanza 4. For the Moon Aries is neutral. Taurus is the place of exaltation, the same is also Moolatrikona and Gemini is a neutral sign.

कर्कटं तु स्वभवंन मित्रक्षेत्रं तु सिंहभं ।
कन्यामित्रं तस्य भवनं तुला समगृहं भवत् ॥ ५ ॥

Stanza 5. Cancer is the own house, Leo and Virgo are friendly signs and Libra is neutral.

वृश्चिकं तु समक्षेत्रं नीचरशिरपिस्मृता ।
शरासनम् समगृहं मकरस्समगृहं भवेत् ॥ ६ ॥

Stanza 6. Scorpio is the place of debilitation as well as a neutral sign and Sagittarius and Capricorn are neutral.

कुम्भक्रृष तु समक्षेत्रं मीनस्स्यान्सम मन्दिरम् ।
विधोग्रहाणां गणनात्वेवं प्रोक्ताच सूरिभि: ॥ ७ ॥

Stanza 7. Aquarius and Pisces are neutral. So have said the learned in Astrology as regards the Moon's relationship with the signs.

MARS — अथ कुज:

कुजस्य मेष स्वक्षेत्रं मूलकोणं तथैव च ।
वृषभं शत्रुभवनं मिथुनंत्वरिमन्दिरम् ॥ ८ ॥

Stanza 8. For Mars Aries is both own house and Moolatrikona, Taurus and Gemini are inimical.

कर्कटं नीचराशिश्च मित्रक्षेत्रमुदाहृतम् ।
सिंहक्रष मित्रभवनम् कन्या शत्रुगृहं भवेत् ॥ ९ ॥

Stanza 9. Cancer is the place of debilitation and a friendly sign, Leo is friendly and Virgo is inimical.

तुला शत्रुगृहंप्रोक्तं वृश्चिक स्वगृहं भवेत् ।
धनुमित्रगृहंप्रोक्तं मकरं शत्रुमन्दिरम् ॥ १० ॥

Stanza 10. Libra is inimical Scorpio is his own sign, Sagittarius is friendly, and Capricorn is inimical.

मकरंचोच्च राशिस्यत्कुम्भशत्रु गृहं भवेत् ।
मीनंतु मित्रक्षेत्रंस्यात्कुजस्यैव वदन्ति: हि ॥ ११ ॥

Stanza 11. And Capricorn is the place of evaltation. Aquarius is inimical and Pisces is friendly. So has been said for Mars.

MERCURY — अथ बुध:

बुधस्यजा समक्षेत्रं वृषोमित्रगृहं भवेत् ।
मिथुन स्वगृहं प्रोक्तं कर्कटं तु द्विषद् गृहं ॥ १२ ॥

Stanza 12. For Mercury, Aries is a neutral sign, Taurus is friendly, Gemini is own house and Cancer is inimical.

सिंहक्रष मित्रभवन कन्या स्वक्षेत्रमुच्यते ।
मूलकोणंतुच्चराशि: कन्या सौम्यस्ययोगदा ॥ १३ ॥

Stanza 13. Leo is friendly, Virgo is own house, *Moolatrikona* and place of exaltation.

तुलामित्रं गृहं प्रोक्तं वृश्चिकं सममन्दिरम् ।
धनुमृगौ समक्षेत्रं कुम्भक्रष सममन्दिरम् ॥ १४ ॥

Stanza 14. Libra is friendly, and Scorpio, Sagittarius Capricorn and Aquarius are neutral ones.

मीने समगृहं प्रोक्तं नीचराशिस्तथा भवेत् ।
बुधस्य गृहगणनात्वेवं प्रोक्ता तु सूरिभिः ॥ १५ ॥

Stanza 15. Pisces is neutral and place of debilitation. So have the learned in Astrology assigned Mercury's relationship with signs.

JUPITER — अथ गुरुः

गुर्रोर्मेषं मित्रगृहं वृषभस्त्वरिमन्दिरम् ।
मिथुनं शत्रुभवनमुच्चस्थानं तु कर्कटम् ॥ १६ ॥

Stanza 16. For Jupiter Aries is friendly Taurus and Gemini are inimical and Cancer is the place of exaltation.

तदेव मित्रभवनं सिंहभं मित्रमन्दिरम् ।
कन्या तुले शत्रुगृहे वृश्चिकं मित्रमन्दिरम् ॥ १७ ॥

Stanza 17. Cancer and Leo are friendly, Virgo and Libra are inimical and Scorpio is friendly.

धनुस्थानं मूलकोणं स्वक्षेत्रचामिधीयते ।
मकरं नीचराशिनु समक्षेत्रमुदाहृतम् ॥ १८ ॥

Stanza 18. Saggittarius is Moolatrikona and own house, Capirocorn is the place of debilitation, and is also neutral.

कुम्भराशि समक्षेत्रं मीनं स्वभवनं भवेत् ।
गुरौ गृहाणां गणनात्वेवं प्रोक्ता तु सूरिभिः ॥ १९ ॥

Stanza 19. Aquarius is neutral and Pisces is own house. So have said the learned in astrology.

VENUS — अथ शुक्रः

भृगोर्मेषं समक्षेत्रं वृषभं स्वस्य मन्दिरम् ।
मिथुनं मित्रभवनं कर्कटं त्वरिमन्दिरम् ॥ २० ॥

Stanza 20. For Venus, Aries is neutral, Taurus is own house, Gemini is neutral and Cancer is inimical.

सिंहक्रष शत्रुभवनं कन्यानीचं सुहृद्द हम् ।
स्वक्षेत्र मूलकोणं च तुलाप्रोक्ता भृगोस्तथा ॥ २१ ॥

Stanza 21. Leo is enemy's sign, Virgo is friendly and place of debilitation, and Libra is Moolatrikona and own house.

वृश्चिकं तु समक्षेत्रं धनुस्त्वरिगृहं भवेत् ।
मकरं मित्रभवनं कुम्भस्तु सुहृदो गृहम् ॥ २२ ॥

Stanza 22. Scorpio is neutral Sagittarius is inimical, and Capricorn and Aqurius are friendly.

मीनक्रष उच्च तु राशिस्याच्छत्रुक्षेत्रं तथैव च ।
भृगोगृहर्हाणां गणनात्वेवं प्रोक्ता च सूरिभिः ॥ २३ ॥

Stanza 23. Pisces is the sign of exaltation and is also inimical. So have the learned in Astrology said about Venus relationship with the difference signs.

SATURN — अथ शनि:

शनेर्मेषो नीचराशि शत्रु-क्षेत्रमुदाहृतम् ।
वृषभं मिथुने चैव मित्रमुदाहृतम् ॥ २४ ॥

Stanza 24. For Saturn, Aries is the sign of debility and an inimical place, Taurus and Gemini are friendly.

कर्कटं शत्रुभवनं सिंहक्रष शत्रुमन्दिरम् ।
कन्यामित्र गृहतौलितूच्चराशि सुहृद्ध्रुहम् ॥ २५ ॥

Stanza 25. Cancer is inimical as also Leo Virgo is friendly and Libra is friendly as well as the sign of exaltation.

वृश्चिकं शत्रुभवनं धनुस्समगृहं भवेत् ।
मकरं स्वभवनं कुम्भ: स्वागारं मूलकोणकम् ॥ २६ ॥

Stanza 26. Scorpio is inimical, Sagittarius is neutral, Capricorn is own house. Aquarius is Moolatrikona, as well as own house.

मीनक्रषेतु समक्षेत्रमित्येवं निर्णय: ॥ २७ ॥

Stanza 27. Pisces is a neutral sign. So are the various signs disposed.

RAHU — अथ राहु:

वृषभस्तूच्चराशिराहो प्रोक्ते तु सूरिभि: ।
मिथुनं कर्कटं चैव मूलकोणमिति श्रुतम् ॥ २८ ॥

Stanza 28. For Rahu Taurus is the place of exaltation, Gemini and Cancer are Moolatrikonas.

वृक्षभं मित्रभवनं कन्या स्वभवनं भवेत् ।
उच्चस्थानस्थ राहोस्तु दायकालो हि राजद: ॥ २९ ॥

Stanza 29. Aries is friendly and Virgo is own house. Rahu when exalted gives political power and fame in his Dasa.

KETHU — अथ केतो:

केतो स्वभवनं मीनतुलामित्रस्य मन्दिरम् ।
कुम्भकीटैतूच्चराशि मूलकोणौ धनुमृगौ ॥ ३० ॥

Stanza 30. For Kethu Pisces is own house, Libra is friendly, Acquarius is own house, Scorpio is the place of exaltation and Sagittarius and Capircorn are Moolatrikona places.

NOTES

The stanzas are simple and can be easily understood and therefore I have given no explanations. The author has assigned friendly places for Rahu and Kethu. Kethu is given ownership over 2 signs and 2 signs are also given for Moolatrikona. Similarly, two signs are given for Moolatrikona for Rahu.

CONCLUSION

I have endeavoured to make the translation as simple and complete as possible. I am sure that after a careful perusal of the translation and the notes my esteemed readers will be highly benefitted. The translation was concluded on Friday 10th September 1943 at 8 p.m. (New IST) at Bangalore when the planetary positions were as follows.

A careful consideration of the above chart (Kundali) should suggest that the book will have a very good reception in the hands of the public especially because Ascendantdhipathi and Mercury are exalted and the

Sun and Venus are in the 6th, Kethu in the 11th and Mars in the 3rd.

		Mars	Saturn			Mars	Merc.
Ascdt.							
	Chart No. 61 RASI		Rahu Jupit.		NAVAMSA		Rahu
Kethu Moon			Sun Venus	Jupit. Moon Kethu			
			Merc.		Sun Saturn		Venus Ascdt.

The End

Index of Technical Terms

Alankara	— Prosody
Alpayu	— Short Life
Amla	— Sour Taste
Angas	— Limbs, Parts.
Apoklimas	— Succeedent Houses.
Aristha	— Misfortune
Ayurbhava	— 8th house
Ayush Karaka	— Indicator of Longevity
Badarayana	— Vyas, the famous Maharshi
Balarishta	— Infant Mortality
Bhava	— House
Bhagya Yoga	— Fortunate combination
Bhagyavahana Yoga	— Combinations bringing paraphernalia and Vehicle
Bhratru Bhava	— 3rd House
Bhratru Karaka	— Indicator of brothers, Mars
Bhukti	— Sub Period
Budha	— Mercury
Budha Dasa	— Period of Budha (Mercury)

Brahma	— Creator, the first of the Hindu Trinity
Brahma Sutras	— Philosophical aphorisums composed by Vyasa
Brihat Jataka	— Famous work on Astrology by Varaha Mihira
Brihat Jataka Yoga	— A Yoga mentioned in Brihat Jataka
Chandra	— The Moon
Chandra Dasa	— The Period of Moon
Chandra Mangala Yoga	— Moon-Mars conjunction or mutual aspect
Chandas	— Rhetoric
Dasa	— Period
Dasa Chidra	— The end of a Dasa
Dhana Bhava	— 2nd House
Dhana Yoga	— Combination for wealth
Dhanur Lagna	— Sagittarius Rising
Dharma Karmadhipa Yoga	— Conjunction between 9th and 10th lord.
Dwirdwadasa	— Planets disposed in the 2nd and 12th from each other

Index of Technical Terms

Gajakesari Yoga	— Mutual disposition of the Moon and Jupiter in quadrants
Grandi Roga	— A disease considered as fatal
Guru Dasa	— The period of Jupiter
Gnana	— Knowledge
Guru Chandala Yoga	— Jupiter-Rahu conjunction
Guru Mangala Yoga	— Conjunction of Jupiter and Mars
Jataka Chandrika	— An astrological treatise
Jyotisha	— Astrology
Kalathra Bhava	— 7th House
Kanya Ascendant	— Virgo rising
Karaka	— Indicator
Karma	— Action, Profession
Karma Bhava	— 10th House
Karma Karaka	— Jupiter
Karkataka	— Cancer
Kashaya	— Mixed taste
Kavya	— Poetry
Kedara Yoga	— A kind of Yoga
Kendra	— Quadrant
Kendradhipathi	— Lord of a quadrant
Karelaeeya	— An ancient astrological treatise

Kethu	—	Dragon's Tail
Khahi	—	Astringent
Khara	—	Hot
Mars	—	Mars
Kumbha	—	Aquarius
Kutumba	—	Family
Labha Bhava	—	11th House
Lagna	—	Ascendant
Lagna Yoga	—	A combination formed by the Position of planets in the Ascendant
Lagnadhipathi	—	Lord of Ascendant
Lavana	—	Saltish
Lomasa	—	An ancient Indian Astronomer
Madhuram	—	Sweet
Madhyayus	—	Middle Age
Maha Raja	—	A King or Ruler
Maha Raja Yogas	—	Combinations for Royalty
Maha Rishi	—	A great sage
Makara	—	Capricorn
Maraka	—	Death of death inflicting
Matru Bhava	—	4th House
Mesha Ascendant	—	Aries rising as Ascendant

Index of Technical Terms

Pisces (Meena) Ascendant	— Pisces rising as Ascendant
Misram	— Mixed
Mithuna	— Gemini
Moksha	— Emancipation
Moolathrikona	— Position similar to exaltation
Mrityu Karaka	— Indicator of death
Navamsa	— 1/9th Division of sign
Neecha	— Debilitation
Neecha Bhanga Raja Yoga	— A combination paliating the debilitation
Nirdhana Yoga	— Combination for poverty.
Nirukta	— *A treatise expounding how Vedas are to be interpreted.* Supposed to be composed by Rishi Yaska
Panaparas	— Succeedent Houses
Parasara	— A great sage and astrologer of Ancient India
Parivarthana Yoga	— Exchange of houses or signs
Pitru Bhava	— 9th House
Pitru Karaka	— The Sun
Poornayus	— Full Life

Prakrithi	—	Nature
Puranic	—	Stories of great heroes of Ancient India
Rahu	—	Dragon's Head or Caput
Rajasa	—	*Virtues of "Nobility"— "Royalty".*
Rasas	—	Tastes
Sani	—	Saturn
Sani Bhukti	—	Sub period of Saturn
Sankhya Yogas	—	Certain combinations Technically known as 'numerical Yogas'..
Sarvartha Chintamani	—	A famous work on Astrology.
Satkarma	—	Good actions or deeds
(Satru) Saturn Bhava	—	6th House
Satwikaguna	—	Pious nature
Simha Ascendant	—	Leo as ascendant
Subha	—	Good, benefic
Subha Parivarthana	—	Auspicious exchange of places
Sudra	—	The 4th caste in Hinduism
Sukra Dasa	—	Period of Venus
Sri Rama	—	The Hero of Ramayana
Tarka	—	Logic
Thamasa	—	Evil Nature

Index of Technical Terms

Thanu Bhava	— 1st House
Thanu Karaka	— Sun
Thrikona	— Trine
Thrikonadhipathi	— Lord of a Trine
Thula Ascendant	— Libra as ascendant
Upachayas	— 3rd, 6th, 10th and 11th houses
Upa Veda	— Treatise based on Vedas, e.g., Astrology, Ayurveda
Vahana	— Vehicle Conveyance
Vahana Karaka	— Venus
Vibana Sthana	— 4th House
Vedas	— Ancient Learning considered As Divine Revelations
Vedangas	— Limbs of the Vedas e.g., Astrology grammar etc
Vedanta	— A class of philosophy
Vidya	— Knowledge, Learning
Vimshottar	— A Dasa based on constellations
Vishnu	— The second God amongst the Hindu Trinity
Scorpio Ascendant	— Scorpio as Ascendant
Vrishaba Ascendant	— Taurus as Ascendant
Vyaya Bhava	— 12th House

Yoga	—	(1) a particular combination of planets and signs (2) Benefic results
Yoga	—	Planet giving rise to a special combination